The best of
Helen
Creighton

The best of
Helen Creighton

Selected & Introduced by
Rosemary Bauchman

LANCELOT PRESS
HANTSPORT, NOVA SCOTIA

ISBN 0-88999-378-5
Published 1988
 Second printing December 1988
Cover design: Robert Pope

LANCELOT PRESS LIMITED
Hantsport, Nova Scotia
Office and production facilities situated on Highway No. 1,
$^1/_2$ mile east of Hantsport.

4

Acknowledgements

The author and publisher gratefully acknowledge permission to quote:

Excerpts from *Folklore of Lunenburg County, Nova Scotia; Bluenose Ghosts; Bluenose Magic* and *A Life In Folklore*, all by Helen Creighton. "Broken Ring Song" and "Cherry Tree Carol" from *Traditional Songs From Nova Scotia* and "Drimindown" from *Maritime Folk Songs*, all collected by Helen Creighton. Reprinted by permission of McGraw-Hill Ryerson Limited.

"Farewell To Nova Scotia" collected by Helen Creighton is used by permission of Gordon V. Thompson Music.

"The Red Mantle" collected by Helen Creighton from *Folksongs From Southern New Brunswick* is used by permission of The National Museum of Canada.

"The Blackbird Song," "Cecilia," music for "The Sauerkraut Song," "The Destitute Family and Mr. Locke" and "Witch Story," all collected by Helen Creighton and used by her permission and that of the Helen Creighton Collection of the Public Archives of Nova Scotia.

Thanks are also due to Mr. William Mont for use of the Devil's Island photogaph, to Mr. Graham Lavers for permission to use the photograph of Dr. Creighton, Clary Croft and Mary Sparling, to Mr. George Georgakakos for use of the photograph of Dr. Creighton and group at Nova Scotia

Symphony Concert reception in 1987. Also to the Helen Creighton Collection of P.A.N.S. for supplying all the other photographs.

Finally, warmest thanks to Roy Bauchman for transcribing the music, to Clary Croft, Contract Archivist of the Helen Creighton Collection, P.A.N.S., for his invaluable help in guiding the author through mountains of fascinating material. Above all, deep gratitude to Dr. Helen Creighton herself for her interest in and approval of this project and generous permission to use her material.

Contents

Introduction

"When I grow up I want to write a book. If I could write just one book I'd be so happy."

Helen Creighton was a young teenager, a student at Halifax Ladies' College, when she voiced that ambition. At that time her imagination could not have encompassed the number of books she would write or the realization that all those books would only be a fraction of her life's work, in truth but a by-product of her main endeavour. She knew nothing then of folklore and music, had no inkling that she would devote her time to collecting and preserving the cultural heritage of her region. This life work was almost providentially timed, beginning, as it did, before radio became the entertainment centre of every home; radio, which supplanted the natural inclination of people to entertain themselves. It had long been the custom at the close of the day to sing around the piano in the parlour, to jig and sing along with a visiting fiddler in the kitchen, or to huddle around the fire while an aged storyteller weaved an enchantment.

The people then didn't know it — Helen Creighton didn't realize it, but they were at the end of a time, an end to the recounting of ancient tales and the singing of songs so old their origin was lost; an end to the almost ritual handing down of the accumulated knowledge and beliefs of ancestors from parents to children. First radio, then television, dispensed information and entertainment to all, resulting in a drab uniformity, a leveling of cultural tastes and interests as individual traditions, songs and experiences were almost blotted out. It is only thanks to a dedicated few, such as Helen Creighton, that our folk songs and folklore were rescued from oblivion.

Mary Helen Creighton was born on September 5, 1899, the sixth and youngest child of Halifax businessman, Charles Edward Creighton and his wife, the former Alice Terry of Kentville. Helen entered the world on the threshold of a new century, one which was to usher in unimaginable changes; her childhood was spent in a vastly different world from the one inhabited by today's children. It was a world of family closeness, in which, as the youngest, she was loved and protected, not only by her parents, but by her four older brothers (her only sister was permanently handicapped as a result of an accident in childhood). Helen has happy memories of picnics and camping, skating and swimming, of a blissful feeling of security as she walked along hand in hand with her father, whom she loved dearly. He was a very special person in her life always, her guide, counsellor and friend, the ultimate authority.

Apart from a life-threatening attack of pneumonia when she was four, Helen was a robust child; her brothers set a standard she strove to emulate, so that she was able to swim across Lake Micmac and back without stopping, at a very early age. She remembers being able to row the boat on her sixth birthday. Her favourite time was winter when she enjoyed sleighing, tobogganing and skating with the rest of the family and friends.

Her school burned down and this became a turning point in her life, as her mother decided she should enter Halifax Ladies' College as a boarder. This proved to be a happy experience where she made many lifelong friends and discovered the urge to write. She entered her stories and poems in competitions and was elated when she occasionally won a prize. When she was due to graduate, her brother Mac, then in London, England, had a dress made for her to wear at the ceremony. "It was a beautiful dress," she recalled, "white crepe-de-chine, much too elaborate, really, but I loved it."

Soon after the Halifax explosion of 1917, Helen, at eighteen, became anxious to try her wings; consequently she became a driver for the air force. She drove an ambulance in

Toronto until the war ended. "The ambulance was a large vehicle, they had to put blocks on the clutch and brake so that I could reach. I don't remember that you could put the seat forward or backward, I think there was just one position. We had to do a double clutch — "

Thus experienced, in 1920 she was invited to drive an ambulance in a Red Cross Caravan which was set up to travel around Nova Scotia, taking medical services to remote places. The roads were unpaved and there were no guardrails. "When you're young life's full of adventure," Dr. Creighton reminisced. "They wouldn't let me drive over Smokey, and I was mortally wounded; I don't think they thought I couldn't handle it, but feared that the ambulance could very well break down and we might be out until all hours of the night — there was more protection for women in those days — "

Apparently she had no premonition that the Red Cross safari through Nova Scotia foreshadowed many such expeditions off the beaten track later in her life.

Contact with people in need of assistance led Helen to think she should go into social work so she enrolled at the University of Toronto to take the necessary course. However, after several intensive months her health broke down; the sturdy little girl had vanished, leaving a delicate young woman with a heart murmur. She learned that she must pace herself, rest a lot and never over-exert herself. Social service was obviously too strenuous, so she reluctantly gave up that idea.

Despondent and lacking direction, she was cheered by an invitation from brother Mac to visit him in Mexico; she accordingly set out on a long, complicated journey by boat and train. She spent a year in Mexico, the first few months enjoying a totally new social whirl as the guest of Mac and his wife. Finding the altitude of Mexico City too taxing, she found a position as a teacher in Gaudalajara. Here she taught English and other subjects to six girls only a few years younger than she was.

There was much of interest in this colourful country and her pen was soon busy recording it. She sent her articles and stories to newspapers and magazines back home. It was a thrill to see her words in print and to be paid for them!

When she returned to Dartmouth she took her children's stories and poems to radio station CHNS which had just been set up, and obtained the position of radio 'aunt,' entertaining children over the air. She thinks she may have been the first radio aunt in Canada. That was in 1926. She became widely known through this work and soon afterwards was invited to join the Canadian Authors Association. Accepting this invitation had far-reaching consequences; she made many friends among like-minded people, friends who made helpful suggestions and were able to steer her in an appropriate direction; she travelled all across the country and to Great Britain for the conferences. Today she is the Honorary Life President of this prestigious national association of writers.

Helen became aware of the bounty of material for stories in her native province. She went to see Dr. Henry Munro, superintendent of Education and asked for advice. At his suggestion she began seeking folk songs (see excerpt from *A Life in Folklore*). At that time (1928) she said, "I had never sung a folk song, I didn't know what a folk song was."

She was to find a wealth of them practically on her own doorstep, at Eastern Passage, Chebucto Head and Devil's Island, which lies just off Eastern Passage at the mouth of Halifax Harbour. Uninhabited now, this small island was home then to the Henneberrys and a number of related families. Separated from the mainland, they entertained themselves and knew many old songs, tales of shipwreck, drownings, pirates and buried treasure, which they willingly related to her. She was a welcome visitor from the first.

It was uphill work in the beginning; she learned not to discuss it with her friends. "People thought I was crazy, going out collecting old songs, they couldn't see the value of it at all."

It could not have been easy for a young woman to go alone to the homes of fishermen and country folk, to introduce herself and her purpose and then to persuade a bashful performer to sing a song, or play a tune on his fiddle. She always maintained a friendly formality, addressing the singers as Mr. or Mrs. So-and-So. This seemed to be a more professional approach than today's first-name familiarity. Helen had great respect for all her singers and appreciated their efforts to remember words and tunes, to have newly recalled songs ready when she came. There were no tape recorders then, and being no musician, she had problems in transcribing the music correctly. She took infinite pains, acquiring a melodeon which she used to transport by wheelbarrow on Devil's Island over the rocky, uneven paths to the houses of the singers.

From songs to stories is a short step; indeed, quite often, when the voices got too tired to sing any more, they switched to tales, with ghost stories being the favourites. A few of those were obviously fabrications designed to entertain or to scare, but some of the simply told supernatural happenings seemed to find an echo in her own experience, for she apparently had psychic ability, sometimes sensing or seeing things not observed by others. "I often get directives," she said, "something will tell me to go a certain way, I do so and find I have avoided trouble or had a narrow escape."

Relaxed by her quiet, friendly manner and flattered by her genuine interest, the people soon began to regard Helen as a friend and would direct her to others who might know songs or ballads forgotten by everyone else. It was long, painstaking work, the travelling and collecting in the summers and the sorting and sifting in the winters. The organizing, typing and indexing of the material followed; it was a huge collection at the end of four years, but finally, in 1932, it was all in order and her first book, *Songs and Ballads From Nova Scotia* was published. Over the years it has been followed by over a dozen other books.

Bluenose Ghosts, first published in 1957, has, perhaps, become her best-known work. It is a best-seller many times over, with thirteen printings. Helen told me, "One reason that I wrote *Bluenose Ghosts* was hoping that it would help people to realize that there is a life after death. I feel so sorry for people who think this is the end, who have trouble believing there is anything else; I like to give people hope."

Between *Songs and Ballads* and *Bluenose Ghosts* two other books of folk songs were published, as well as *Folklore of Lunenburg County, Nova Scotia*. In that period there was also the tempting invitation to become a radio announcer in the late 1930s, an offer which she declined, and a two-year span from 1939 to 1941 when she became Dean of Women at King's College in Halifax, a position she enjoyed, valuing it for her contact with the students. "It was a good experience," she commented.

The years became ever busier; in 1936 she spent a month lecturing in New York. That was followed by a speaking engagement in Montreal. From there she went to Ottawa and met Mr. Gladstone Murray, head of the CBC. Seizing the opportunity, Helen asked him if there was any possibility of a programme featuring some of the folk songs she had collected. To her delight this idea was favourably received and she wound up making ten half-hour broadcasts, using several of her original singers. It was so popular it was repeated.

The collecting went on in tandem with whatever other involvement had arisen. Before the war she was occasionally accompanied by Doreen Senior, a music teacher who came over from England in the holidays, and helped wonderfully by transcribing the music on the spot. Sometimes Helen's mother went with her, or her father. Her parents were always most interested and supportive of her work, which was constantly expanding.

Her awareness of the many ethnic strains in the province increased. As time went on she obtained a wealth of both songs and folklore from the German community in Lunenburg; lively Scottish music and tales from Cape Breton; Acadian material from the south shore around Yarmouth (a book of Acadian folksongs is pending publication); the Black community and the Micmac Indians made wonderful contributions; in the Shelburne area and parts of the Annapolis Valley she interviewed descendants of Loyalists. She collected many songs in southern New Brunswick and Prince Edward Island, many with the added interest of words in Gaelic from Scotch or Irish ancestry. Material of English origin cropped up everywhere.

The 1940s saw many changes in Helen's life; her mother, who had been ailing for some time, died in the spring of 1941. Helen was left to care for her father and sister Lilian at "Evergreen," the family home in Dartmouth. It was wartime and the Halifax-Dartmouth area was crowded with servicemen and their families needing accommodation. Helen was inspired to convert the upstairs of the house into flats, consequently had a series of tenants over the years, many of whom became long-time friends. It was always sheer joy to be with her father, but sadly, his health deteriorated, and to her great sorrow, he passed away in October, 1943.

Helen had worked for some years under the auspices of the National Museum of Canada, who published some of her songs. Now, in 1943, the Library of Congress provided her with recording equipment. This consisted of a heavy machine which used batteries for electricity, a microphone on a stand, blank acetate discs and a sapphire needle for cutting the grooves. "When assembled it was formidable . . ."

This was another milestone as she learned how to use the equipment, how to record her singers. Conveying and setting up the heavy equipment was a challenge in itself, but she was soon able to manage it successfully. It was a big step forward from the melodeon in the wheelbarrow, a long way from the dots she had marked on paper in her first attempts to transcribe a tune. She notes how easy it is for collectors since the advent of tape recorders. She acquired her first tape recorder in 1949.

All too often artists, writers, researchers, people who work in solitude, receive no recognition until it is too late. For a long time Helen Creighton felt she was working in a vacuum and wondered wryly if it were true that a prophet had no honour in his own country. This thought often struck her as she listened to programmes of folk music on the local media when nothing she had discovered was ever mentioned, although she occasionally heard one of her songs on the national network, or even from the United States or England. "It wasn't until Ian Slanders did an article in the 1950s that the average person really comprehended that there was something in this."

Then Clary Croft approached her, seeking local material; in a short time she presented him with a list of over one hundred songs. Since then this talented folk singer has featured her songs, singing with his guitar. In addition, for some years Clary has also been occupied cataloguing and organizing the "Dr. Helen Creighton Collection" at the Public Archives of Nova Scotia.

1957 was the year when the name of Helen Creighton became a household word. She was featured in a television documentary; *Bluenose Ghosts* was published and became extremely popular; Mount Allison University made her an Honorary Doctor of Laws. This was but the first of six honorary doctorates she received. The others were conferred by St. Mary's University, Laval University, King's College, St. Francis Xavier University and Mount Saint Vincent University.

Since then the honours have flooded in; she greatly prizes the one she received in 1968 when she was named a Fellow of the American Folklore Society. "... you can't go any higher in folklore on this continent."

In this area of her prime interest she was thrilled to receive a beautifully bound book of testimonial letters from the folklore societies of illustrious institutions (principally universities in the United States) which was presented by the North-Eastern Folklore Society. The Folklore Association of Canada designated her "Distinguished Folklorist of 1981." She was made a Fellow of the American Folklore Society in 1968 and a Fellow of the Haliburton Club, Halifax 1967.

In 1966 Dartmouth Kiwanis named her their Citizen of the Year. She received a medal from the Canadian Music Council; a Testimonial Dinner was given in her honour by the Nova Scotia Government in 1974. She was a recipient of The Order of Canada in 1976 and named Dartmouth Citizen of the Year in 1978. She was named for the Cultural Life Award by the Nova Scotia Choral Foundation and made an Honorary Life member of the Writers' Federation of Nova Scotia. Those are only some of the honours.

A musical play about her life entitled *The Collector* was written by J. Frederick Brown and staged at Mount St. Vincent University by Sister Margaret Young. The Dartmouth Choral Society honoured her with a programme of her songs in May, 1986 and saluted her again in June,1987 with a musical presentation at the Canadian Authors national conference in Halifax.

On November 20, 1987 a wonderful tribute to Helen Creighton was staged at the Rebecca Cohn auditorium in Halifax. Participating in the presentation were the Dalhousie

Chorale, Symphony Nova Scotia, conductor Dr. Walter Kemp, singers Mary Kelly and Clary Croft, all combining their talents under the inspired direction of arranger Scott MacMillan, to salute Canada's First Lady of Folklore with a choice selection of the folk songs she had collected. It was with a full heart that she commented afterwards, "Many musicians have made arrangements of our music, but none with the magic of Scott MacMillan."

The following passages from Helen Creighton's writings were selected to illustrate the diversity, scope and human interest of her folklore, just as a concert featuring a dozen of her songs would give an insight into the wide range of the folk music she collected. This small volume offers but a taste of what is available in the original books; it is hoped that this taste will stimulate the appetite of readers and send them back for more.

All of Helen Creighton's books and papers are preserved in the Dr. Helen Creighton Collection of the Public Archives of Nova Scotia, ensuring that future generations will have access to the fruits of her endeavour.

Rosemary Bauchman
January, 1988

Books by Helen Creighton

Songs and Ballads from Nova Scotia, 1932, J.M. Dent & Sons, Toronto, and 1966, Dover Publications, New York.

Twelve Folksongs from Nova Scotia (with Doreen Senior), 1940, Novello & Company, Ltd., London. Published under the auspices of the National Council of Education of Canada.

Folklore of Lunenburg County, 1950, National Museum of Canada, Ottawa.

Traditional Songs from Nova Scotia (with Doreen Senior), 1950, The Ryerson Press, Toronto. Reprinted 1987.

Bluenose Ghosts, 1957, The Ryerson Press, Toronto. Thirteen printings.

Maritime Folk Songs, 1961, The Ryerson Press, Toronto. Paperback edition, 1972, McGraw-Hill Ryerson, Toronto. Reprinted 1987.

Eight Folktales from Miramichi (with Edward D. Ives), 1962. *Northeast Folklore IV*, University of Maine, Orono.

Gaelic Songs in Nova Scotia, (with Calum MacLeod). 1964, National Museum of Canada, Ottawa.

Bluenose Magic, 1968, The Ryerson Press, Toronto. Reprinted 1970. Paperback, 1978, McGraw-Hill Ryerson, Toronto.

Folksongs From Southern New Brunswick, 1971, Canadian Centre for Folk Culture Studies, National Museum of Man, Ottawa.

With a Heigh-Heigh-Ho, Stories and Verse for Children, illustrated by Bill Johnson, 1986, Nimbus Publishing Limited, Halifax, N.S.

A Life in Folklore, 1975, McGraw-Hill Ryerson, Toronto.

Excerpts from

Folklore of Lunenburg County, Nova Scotia

Folklore of Lunenburg County, Nova Scotia, first published in 1950, was Helen Creighton's first book of folklore; it was preceded by two books of ballads and folk songs. Collecting folk songs was always Dr. Creighton's main purpose, the tales seemed incidental and were often noted out of politeness towards the people who wished to relate stories when their singing voices failed. Helen kept them, thinking vaguely that she might be able to do something with them some day.

When visiting in Chester in October, 1944, a friend urged her to visit Tancook Island, a large polliwog-shaped island which lies at the mouth of Mahone Bay. Armed with her suitcase and a list of possible lodging places, Helen left Chester by boat on a bitterly cold day and crossed seven miles of rough sea to the island, which was renowned for its sauerkraut (It has since gained a reputation for its apple dolls, an old European craft revived, which has become very popular in recent times). She was fortunate to find accommodation at a house where a Rev. and Mrs. Bezanson lived nearby. They had an interest in folk tales so Helen went with them on their visits to residents of the island for three days, and heard many fascinating stories and snippets of ancient wisdom.

Ethnically, Lunenburg County is unique in Nova Scotia. It was originally settled by German Protestants about the year 1752; with them came a sprinkling of Swiss immigrants and French Huguenots. These people called themselves Dutch (actually a corruption of Deutsch), and their descendants form a large percentage of the population of the county in the present day. Although the German language has largely been lost, these "South Shore Dutchmen" speak with a very distinctive accent and are, for the most part, of necessity, lumbermen, fishermen and boat builders as well, consequently their lore is of crops and animals, the seasons, weather, seas, tides and skies.

Leaving Tancook Island, Helen stayed on in the area for six weeks, collecting tales in Chester, Mahone Bay and points between. She found few folk songs since the original German songs had not been translated and as the younger people lost the language the songs were forgotten. However, there were a few indigenous songs, such as the two included here relating to the making of sauerkraut. The folklore, however, was another matter; this area was particularly rich in old tales and customs. Women at spinning and rug-hooking parties exchanged all manner of tales about ghosts, witches, treasure, pirates, recipes, crafts, games and home remedies. They had their own superstitions, pet sayings, proverbs, riddles and anecdotes.

Those six information-packed weeks yielded enough material for a good-sized volume. It took her the next four years to classify her notes and write the book.

Folklore of Lunenburg County, Nova Scotia has great popular appeal as well as being invaluable to scholars. Every item is numbered for reference and place of origin given. There are footnotes, a Bibliography and an Appendix of folk dances.

Dr. Creighton told me, "Of all the books I've done, this gave me the most enjoyment."

Treasure

Nova Scotia is almost an island, and there is scarcely a place along the whole coastline where stories are not told about Captain Kidd and his treasure. The belief that it is here colours the lives and actions of many people who hope one day to unearth it. From Yarmouth to Cape North there is a succession of bays and inlets, but none of these could have been more tempting to a pirate than Mahone Bay with its 365 islands, "one for every day in the year." Oak Island is the best known; it has attracted international interest and many thousands of dollars have been spent in excavations over a long period of years. The mystery of the man-made supports that were found under the ground has never been solved, but their presence stimulates the general belief in the reality of the buried treasure.

Although to date nothing has occurred to prove that Captain Kidd came here, the supposition that he may have done so is supported by the fact that treasure has been dug up from time to time, although not in fabulous amounts. It is well known that sea captains used to carry currency in gold and silver and that upon occasion, rather than risk losing it at sea, they would find a suitable place ashore and bury it, planning to come back for it later. If they were prevented from coming, it remained there and may be there to this day.

The finding of treasure, however, is not as simple as it sounds, for there is much supernatural belief behind it. In fact it is often difficult to get local men to work on excavations because they have always heard such awesome stories all their lives. A few of the braver souls have scorned fear when treasure appeared, and have lived in comparative comfort ever since. People who secure money from such unexpected sources never talk about it, although their neighbours always know they have it. In sparsely settled districts it is not easy to keep secrets.

As many of the superstitions connected with treasure are European in origin, I have divided my material into five motifs. These explain: (1) the reason why a ghost is always on hand to guard buried treasure; (2) why lights indicate the place where treasure lies; (3) how treasure disappears if a word is spoken while digging, or if the treasure is not taken away the moment it is found; (4) how people are led to buried treasure through dreams; and (5) stories of actual treasure trove.

Ghosts Prevent Men From Raising Treasure
In the old days when a pirate buried his treasure he'd pick out a man, cut off his head, and put it in the hole with the treasure to watch it. *Mahone Bay.*

Captain Kidd drew lots to get watchmen for his treasure — *Riverport.*

In Mahone Bay a man was going home one night and he saw a little fire. He went to investigate and it was a lot of clam shells and they were all fiery. He picked a handful up and put them in his pocket. When he came home he went to show them, and when he reached his hand in his pocket he hauled out a lot of double loons. They were Spanish silver — *Lunenburg.*

A chest of gold with a lot of double loons was found this year at Port Medway. There had been a light above the place where it was found. They took it to the bank and the bank gave them credit for a lot of money. — *Lunenburg.*

Speaking Causes Seeker to Lose Treasure
I heard a crowd getting a treasure once and they just got it up out of the ground when somebody said, "We got it," and it disappeared out of their hands. — *Lunenburg.*

There is a low clump of trees at the end of the land where a light comes up. The people living around there all thought there must be money buried there, so one night they all took their lanterns and spades and dug, saying nothing. At last one of them said, "There it is!" and it went away. — *Lunenburg.*

Treasure Discovered Through Dream
People have always dreamt there was treasure buried at Kraut Point. Recently holes have been found dug on Five Houses Hill, one in an oat field. There were tracks in the oat field leading to the water and they were done as though something had been dragged there.

Some other people dreamed that money was buried in a place and one day a stranger walked into one of the houses and fell asleep. Afterwards he told them his dream, and he too had dreamed where the treasure was buried. — *Riverport.*

Treasure Trove

There was a man who heard a pirate say when he buried his gold that no one could get it unless he ploughed with a rooster and harrowed with a hen. So he got the rooster and ploughed, and made a little harrow and harrowed with a hen, and he got the gold. — *Lunenburg.*

One night a man was travelling in Lunenburg and he came to a house and asked the people to get out. They did, and when they came back in the morning they found a big hole dug below the house. The man had dug up the treasure. — *Lunenburg.*

Forerunners

I wasn't married yet, and I was coming home one moonlight night when the snow was on the ground and it was almost as light as day. About 100 yards ahead of me I saw a man get up out of a snowbank, and I thought, "I'm not going to tussle with you," thinking he was drunk. Then I thought, "No, I'll see who it is." As I got nearer I thought it looked like my brother, but I knew that my brother was out courting in another direction and I couldn't understand it. The apparition walked ahead of me 300 yards, and when I got up to him it was 20 yards. He had a brown ulster on and his pipe was in his mouth. I even saw his eyes blink, and then I walked up behind him 3 or 4 yards, and when I went up closer to look at him there was nothing there. He had vanished.

My brother lived with my uncle, and the next morning I told my uncle what had happened and asked him where my brother had been at that time. He said he'd been home in bed because he was sick, so we decided not to tell him anything about it because we thought that seeing him when he wasn't there must be a forerunner and that he was going to die. When he got better I told him, and he said for me to stop because another friend of his had met him in another place that same night.

The evening after it happened I went back to the same place to see if it could happen again, but there was another man there, not an apparition, but a real man this time. He said, "What are you going to do, fight me?" I knew him, so I told him what had happened the night before. He said, "Was he coming towards you or going away from you?" I told him he was going away from me. "Well," he said, "take it from me, that is a sign of a long life for both you and your brother." — *Mahone Bay.*

One day we were sitting down by the river talking and the first thing we heard an awful rushing noise overhead like a span of horses dropping rocks as they went. It was a terrible noise and we couldn't give any account of it. We think now it must have been a forerunner of the aeroplane. — *North River.*

The Restless Dead

Every time a sailor drowns he takes (inhabits) the soul of one of the birds at Ironbound, a sort of Stormy Petrel or Carey's Chicken. The people will not disturb the birds because it would disturb the souls. — *Riverport.*

At Beech Hill a man died and his wife lived on in the house. She said that every night he would come in the bedroom at the regular hour he had done all his life and wind his watch. — *Riverport.*

Female Revenants

The story is told of a man who was rector of the Anglican Church at Annapolis and who was sitting one day in his study when an apparition of a lady in white came to him. The lady asked him to go to a certain house in Halifax at a certain time because his help was needed there. He was startled at the request, but it was so definite that he felt he should go. When he arrived he found that the widow of a fellow clergyman was in great difficulty and he was able to help her.

Some years later the story was told in an officer's mess and the late Rev. Robert Norwood of New York and Hubbards happened to be there. He seemed so interested that the narrator asked him what he thought of the story.

"Oh," he said, "I know it's right because it was my father who saw the apparition." — *Lunenburg.*

'Ghost Haunts House

A woman moved into a house at Lower LaHave that she was told was haunted. One day a neighbour asked her why she always went into a certain room at a certain time with a lamp. She didn't let on that she hadn't been there, but it bothered her along with other things she heard.

One night it got too much for her and she sat up in bed and said, "In the name of God I never hurt anybody, and nobody is ever going to hurt me." There followed a dreadful noise and she never heard anything again. She had laid the ghost. — *Hebbville.*

Ghost Exorcised and Laid

If you see a ghost say, "In the name of the Father, Son and Holy Ghost, what do you want?" and they will answer you if they want anything. If they want anything and tell you about it they will never come back again. There was a girl whose grandfather would appear to her and try to get her to follow him. People said she should have gone with him because he must have wanted to show her something. — *Lunenburg, Mahone Bay, and East River Point.*

Witches

Witches used to put a spell on creeturs, so horseshoes were put over barn doors for luck. A witch can't get into the barn if a horseshoe is up over the door. — *Blandford, North West, Mahone Bay, Lunenburg.*

When I was young I was sleeping upstairs. Every night and every night when I would go to bed the door would open but I couldn't see nothin'. About 2 minutes afterwards it was in the bed, just as if it was a cat or a dog. I used to get up and shut the door and then it would open again. It went on that way for 2 or 3 years, and it used to pull the bedclothes off the bed. Then my uncle said, "I've got a charm for witchcraft," and he took nine letters from the German Bible and he put them on a board backwards and put the board up over the door. From that time it never came again. The witch could go over the board but not under it. There are ten words in English. They mean, "And the word was made flesh and dwelt among us." — *Lunenburg.*

Funerals

This was told at Rose Bay:
They used to have oil lamps where they boiled cod oil, and when anybody died they painted the coffin with cod oil and lamp black. They closed the eyes with cents. Coffins were made here and were covered with cashmere, and if they were specially good they were covered with velvet. The first caskets were all wood without any cover. Babies' coffins were covered with white shirting cotton. It cost $4 to make a coffin. It was carried by handles to the grave, four on each side.

After the funeral they had a wonderful feast and everyone got drunk. They had to have cheese, and as soon as anybody died they got cheese out from Lunenburg. Everybody stayed for the feast and had loaf cake and bread and cheese and wine. The men wore black crepe on their hats with the tails down their backs, and everybody wore black clothes to the funeral.

When grandmother died they put a bedbug in a box to bury with her, and I got the bedbug and let it loose. I was quite young and saw the box and wondered what it was. Children were made to go to the coffin and touch the corpse with the backs of their hands so they wouldn't be scared. The bedbug had been put in the coffin because they thought that if it went with her, all the bedbugs would leave the house.

At North West the poles for carrying the coffin were called death poles, and after the funeral they were put in the dead house (the undertaker's) until wanted again. Here funerals were held in the forenoon because most of the mourners came by horse team and it took them a long time to get there. There was always a funeral cake which was a plain cake with cinnamon but no fruit.

The old funeral rites are still observed at Cornwall, with a great display of weeping and emotion and misery before they leave the house. After the interment everything is changed. Tables are filled with food and there is no further sign of grief.

Memorial Service

In all the 71 years since I started fishing this is the first one I ever remember when there hasn't been a single drowning (1944). One year five vessels were lost with their whole crews, and that meant over a hundred men were drowned. Another year two whole crews went down. At the end of the fishing season when all the fishermen came home from the Banks we have always held a memorial service at the Town Square. People came from Petit Rivière and Tancook and all over the place and the town was packed. This took place towards the last of September or the first of October. People who had lost anybody brought wreaths, and when the service was over they would take all the wreaths to the wharf and they would go aboard a vessel and deposit them in the harbour. This year was the first time we were able to hold a thanksgiving service instead.

In the old days the men would be away for 3 or 4 months at a time, and when the ships came back the women never went

near the wharves. There would have been plenty of talk if they
had. The wives used to look to see if the ship's flag was flying,
and if it was half mast they knew someone had died.

Sauerkraut Song (A)

Now if ye'll only listen to phwat ye spake about
I'm going for to toll you how to make that sauerkraut,
The kraut is not made of leather as effery one supposes
But off that little plant what they call the cabbage roses.

Chorus
>Sauerkraut is bully, I toll you it is fine,
>Me thinks me ought to know 'em for me eats 'em all the
>time.

2. The cabbages are growing so nice as it could be,
    We take 'em and cut 'em up the bigger as a pea,
    Me put 'em in a barrel and me stamp 'em with me feet,
    And we stamp and we stamp for to make 'em nice and
    sweet. *Chorus*

3. Me put in plenty of salt so nice, don't put in no snuff,
    Nor any cayenne pepper nor any of that stuff,
    Me put 'em in the cellar till it begins to smell,
    So help me Christ, me thinks it nice, the Dutchmen like it
    well. *Chorus*

4. When the sauerkraut begins to smell and it can't smell no
    smeller
    We take it from the barrel that's way down in the cellar,
    Me put him in the kettle and it begins to boil,
    So help me we can smell her round for 40,000 miles.
                                                    Chorus
           Sung by Mr. Japeth Dauphinee, Hubbards.

30

Sauerkraut Song (B)

I've just arrived from Tancook
And the folks they are all well,
We have a load of sauerkraut
Which we would like to sell.
We're laying up to Silver's wharf
In the schooner *Pauline Young*,
The summer we go sword fishing,
In the spring we bring our dung.

Come down into the morning
With three dollars in your hand,
I'll sell you a barrel of sauerkraut,
The finest in the land.
Our sauerkraut is lovely,
Our cabbage they are fine,
You people ought to know it
For you eat it all the time.

Before I leave the city
I'll tell you how it's made,
The cabbage is cut up fine
And in the barrel it's laid,
We off with our high toppers
And in the barrel we jump
And with our naked feet
Oh, we smash down the lumps.

Sung at Tancook.

The singer used to get five cents a half barrel for trampling kraut. The men at Tancook were very clean and washed their feet so thoroughly before tramping that the skin was almost scraped off. As children they enjoyed it, but it was hard work. Later they tramped with well-cleansed rubber boots and the next stage was a pounder with a handle. Then they put a weight on the pounder and a rock on the barrel head . . . Methods of making kraut are becoming more modern all the time. For tune see Library of Congress recording.

Remedies

Give peppermint and spearmint tea for colds. — *Rose Bay*.

Use onion poultice for colds. — *Mahone Bay*, *Whynacht's Settlement* and *Tancook*.

For a cold take a good dose of senna and drink peppermint tea. Peppermint is grown here on the island. Senna tea is made by pouring boiling water on the leaves. — *Tancook*.

Drink juniper tea for colds. — *Tancook*.

Salt herring at the feet will cure a cold. — *Bridgewater*.

For colds and coughs steep mullein leaves. — *Bridgewater*.

Use onion poultice for congestion. — *Garden Lots*.

Use sea lilies for cough. — *Rose Bay*.

Teaberry and molasses are good for cough. — *Whynacht's Settlement*.

For cramps in the legs when you go to bed at night turn your shoes upside down with the heels up. — *Mahone Bay*.

This remedy which is also used for rheumatism, may be explained under the head of the transference of the disease, common not only in Germany, but in Mexico, Ireland, Persia and elsewhere. The idea is that the disease is transferred to the floor or earth by turning the shoes upside down.

In Cornwall a charm from the manuscript of a white witch reads as follows: "The cramp is keenless, Mary was sinless when she bore Jesus; let the cramp go away in the name of Jesus."

To cure a man of drink take an eel and put in rum, but don't leave the eel in long enough to die. Then give the rum to the person to drink, but don't tell him about the eel. If he drinks it he will never touch rum again. — *Lunenburg*.

For earache take wool from between the ears of a black sheep and put in your ear. — *Mahone Bay*.

Tie warm tealeaves in a cloth and put over eyes if they are weak or inflamed. — *Garden Lots*.

For fever tie salt herring or salt pork around the neck and leave it overnight between cloths. In the morning the herring will be as hard as a board. — *Lunenburg*.

White balsam is made into a drink and used for fever. — *Rose Bay*.

Sage is used for fever, colds and sore throat. — *Rose Bay*.

Catnip tea and summer savory are used for fever.

To stop a fever put a poultice of flaxseed at the feet. — *Bridgewater*.

If a child has fits we would split an oak tree and put the child in it. If the tree grew the child would get better, but if not, the child would die. — *Blockhouse*.

To make hair grow put sunfish oil on two or three times a week. It is also used to make hair grow over an injury when a horse has a cut. — *East River Point*.

I learned a cure in Annapolis County that is good for indigestion. Before breakfast take a spoonful of the gravel that is put in a bird's cage, and keep doing this for two years. — *East River Point*.

Pour hot water over August flowers and steep. Drink three or four times a day before meals. — *Tancook*.

Sheep tea was used for measles and given to children to drink. It was made of dry droppings from sheep, steeped and strained. — *Indian Point* and *Garden Lots*.

Steep the yellow flower of tansy for regular menses. — *Whynacht's Settlement*.

Drink pennyroyal to bring on menstruation. — *Whynacht's Settlement* and *Garden Lots*.

Use sage or goldenroot as mouth wash when the mouth is sore. — *Garden Lots*.

To cure a sty rub the eyes with a wedding ring. — *Whynacht's Settlement*.

To cure a wart rub with a bean and put the bean under a spout where water will drip on it. As the bean decays the wart will disappear. — *Lunenburg*.

Take half an apple and rub the wart an uneven number of times. You mustn't tell anybody or count the number yourself, but get somebody older than yourself to count. Put the apple under the eave of the roof and as the rain drops the wart will go away. — *Rose Bay*.

Angle worms tied around the waist with string will cure worms in the body. — *Tancook*.

For a spring tonic take Epsom-salts and cream of tartar for 9 alternate mornings. — *Lunenburg.*

Animals

This section on animal lore, . . . takes in all corners of the county. The pig, cattle and lowly ox are the animals referred to, and all are included in the general designation "creetur." There are horses in many places, of course, but the ox is the friend of farmer and fisherman and is a more practical beast of burden over rocky shores and hillsides. A horse is expensive to buy and may fall and break a leg, whereupon he is of no further use to his master. The ox is a slow-moving animal, but sure-footed and dependable. There is as much affection between a Lunenburg county man and his ox as between any other farmer and his horse.

A man with a single ox is said to drive a smiler or jolly ox, and a pair is called a team. There is little variety in their names, for they are practically always known as Spark and Lion, being considered always in pairs. Brown Duke is also used. As one farmer explained it, the off one is on the right and the nigh one is on the left, and they are trained as a sergeant trains his men, and know what their orders mean.

There is a nobility in the appearance of a Lunenburg man bringing his team to town. He walks at their head, long whip in hand, sometimes walking backwards, sometimes forwards, and pride in every line. His oxen have been carefully selected and are very choice, and the vehicle they draw is well built and sturdy. The words used to direct them are unintelligible to the uninitiated ear and are shouted in a loud voice, but if we find them difficult to understand, the trained beast knows every traditional inflexion. Gee, haw, whoa, and a word that sound like huet and means to back, are the words they use. At Mahone Bay the tinkling of the oxen's bells and the whistling of the men as they work provide an unusually pleasant atmosphere.

When the tide is rising kill the creetur and the meat will swell up. If killed in the ebbing tide it will shrink. — *Riverport,*

Upper Kingsburg and Tancook. Kill the pig at the full of the moon. — *Tancook.*

If a cat is poisoned give it warm soda water followed by oil. — *Whynacht's Settlement.*

If the cow has sniffles put tar up her nose. — *Tancook.*

For tooth sickness take soot out of the stove pipe and put it in the cow's mouth and make her set her teeth. Or rub her teeth with soot. — *Tancook* and *East Chester.*

Cows give their milk if they hear music. — *Whynacht's Settlement.*

Weather Lore

Weather lore is largely influenced by the tide, the sun, moon, stars and the direction of the wind . . . To men who make their living on the sea and who have to go out upon the great waters in all seasons, one can readily imagine how eagerly they scan all the natural phenomena to know how they should plan ahead. Some of the few beliefs given here are known everywhere, but it is interesting to note that those that take in the rise and fall of the tides are purely local . . .

Curiously enough, I had never until the year 1945 heard that it was important which way the wind was blowing on March 21 when the sun crossed the equator. That year it came from the northeast, accompanied by a snowstorm, and fulfilled the Lunenburg prophecy . . . that the next three months would be cold and miserable.

If it looks like rain and doesn't rain when the tide is rising, it won't rain that day. — *Riverport.*

The wind won't change until the tide changes. — *Riverport.*

If it rains on the flood it will only be a scud.

If it rains on the ebb you may as well go to bed. — *Riverport.*

When the wind's in the south
The rain's in his mouth. — *Riverport.*

If it blew hard from the northwest, it blows hard for 3 days. — *Riverport.*

If the wind goes down with the sun it comes up with the sun. — *Riverport.*

If the sun crosses the line on March 21 in a northeast wind and a snowstorm, there will be no summer, or three months more of cold weather. — *East Chester.*

If the sun is shut in and streaky it will not be fine. — *Blandford.*

Sun dogs in the evening mean a storm. — *Blandford.*

If the sun sets beautifully on the last Friday of the month, the following month will be fine. — *Mahone Bay* and *Lunenburg.*

If the change of the moon falls on Sunday you are sure to have rain before the week is out. — *North River.*

A milk pad running northeast and southwest means southwest winds (this is the Milky Way). — *Tancook.*

The direction in which a shooting star falls is the direction the wind will blow the next day. — *Lunenburg.*

Green Christmas, full graveyard,
Green Christmas, white Easter. — *Lunenburg.*

On July 15, if Mary goes over the hill and gets her skirts wet it will rain for 40 days. — *Whynacht's Settlement.*

Evening red and morning grey
Will set the traveller on his way,
But evening grey and morning red
Will pour down rain upon his head. — *Lunenburg and Riverport.*

Rainbow at night, sailor's delight,
Rainbow in the morning, sailor's take warning. — *Blandford.*

If your corn bites it is going to rain. — *Lunenburg.*

If the pan on the stove goes dry it is going to rain. — *Riverport.*

Like Friday, like Sunday. — *LaHave.*

If cattle jump around in the evening it is a sign of a storm. — *Whynacht's Settlement.*

Proverbs and Old Sayings

It was a simple matter to collect proverbs and old sayings in Lunenburg County because everybody seemed to know them. Many turned up in ordinary conversation. . .

The meaning behind proverbs is interesting. For instance I had no idea that a dead man's eyes were often kept closed with pennies until I was told that somebody was "Mean enough to steal the pennies off a dead man's eyes." I had heard that the fortunes of a family were inclined to rise and fall, usually in three generations, and found it expressed here as "clogs, carriages, clogs," and "From shirtsleeves to shirtsleeves." This means that a poor or shirtsleeve generation works and lays up a fortune that is soon spent and another generation must take to its shirtsleeves. Many of the proverbs are filled with worldly wisdom, and it is well to remember when one is inclined to be tart that, "Honey catches more flies than vinegar." That is, a pleasant approach is more likely to yield results than an acid one.

Every proverb probably came into being through somebody's wise or witty remark. It struck the popular fancy and spread from one person to another until in time everybody was using it to express a certain idea. By collections made in various places we are able to see how wide the dissemination has been, and in some cases trace the proverb to its source. The changes it has undergone and the way it has been adapted to meet the life of its new home are interesting and important.

In going through collections of proverbs from other places I was astonished to find how many were in common everyday use in the life of my own family. I also discovered that I am more familiar with proverbs from other sources than with these from Lunenburg County, many of which I had never heard before . . .

To charm the heart of a grindstone. — *Mahone Bay.*

A place for everything and everything in its place. — *Riverport.*

If you haven't it in your head you must have it in your heels. — *Riverport.*

A person so worthless he couldn't make a patch for a jib-boom sail for a wheelbarrow. — *Blockhouse.*

As cold as stepmother's breath (cold air from an open door). — *Lunenburg.*

It's no load to carry (if you know how to do a thing it is no burden). — *Lunenburg and Mahone Bay.*

Everything is lovely and the goose is hanging high. — *Lunenburg.*

As supple as an eel. — *Rose Bay.*

Better a small fish than an empty dish. — *Lunenburg.*

A good dinner's better than a fine coat. — *Lunenburg.*

It's not worth two bites of a cherry. — *Tancook.*

One unjust penny eats ten. — *Tancook.*

Nothing pays like weather. — *Riverport.*

What do you think I am, an 8-day clock or a sewing machine? (said when somebody is being hurried along too quickly).

A new broom sweeps clean but an old one knows the corners best. — *Lunenburg.*

Whoever makes love forgets its care. — *Lunenburg.*

What goes against your will doesn't go right. — *Blockhouse.*

Don't swap the devil for a witch. — *Mahone Bay.*

She'd build an ark (or a house) on his head (said of somebody much admired). — *Oakland.*

Take the wool off a sheep's back and put it on a man's (said when the whole process of cloth making is done at home from growing the wool to making the garment). — *Oakland.*

Anecdotes

An old woman, the mother of a large family, came out of a church one morning. The sermon had been on matrimony. When asked what she thought of it she said, "I wish I knew as little about it as he does." — *Tancook.*

One time Sir Thomas Esmond and his wife came out to New Ross shooting. The Roman Catholic priest was a friend of Sir Thomas, and he got John Murphy to guide him. They were staying at our place when John came in pretty well cut (intoxicated). They were having lunch and he sat down and said, "Now, milord, I've shot the moose. All you have to do is go out and fire at it." — *Gold River.*

A Tancook woman went one day to a large town on the main (mainland) and saw this sign: Smith's Manufacturing Company.

"Oh, my," she exclaimed. "I never knew before where all the Smiths came from." — Tancook.

A coloured woman asked a doctor if she could have a baby, and he said if she did it would be a miracle. Her husband asked her what the doctor had said and she said he told her if she had one it would be a mackerel. — *East River Point.*

Two men in the country were talking and one was deaf. He said, "What did you say? Talk a little louder. I harks hard." — *Mahone Bay.*

Tall Tales

A fellow went into the woods for moose and he only had one load of ammunition. He seen the moose and he was getting ready to fire when he heard a noise on one side of him, and he looked and saw a fox. This didn't scare him much, and he was just getting ready to fire on the fox when he heard a noise on the other side of him and he looked and saw a bear.

"What am I going to do now?" he said. "If I fire on the fox the bear will turn on me, and if I fire on the bear the fox will turn on me, and if I fire on them both the moose will turn on me."

Then he heard a noise behind him and he looked and there was a rattlesnake. So he decided to shoot the moose, and when he did the gun exploded and one bit hit the bear and killed the bear. Another hit the fox and killed the fox. The bullet hit the moose and killed it, but the gun knocked the man down and he sat on the rattlesnake and killed it. Now isn't that a good lie? — *Lunenburg.*

An American was travelling with a Canadian and the American was boasting. Everything was bigger and better in the United States. The Canadian got fed up and thought he would go one better, so as they started off to bed he found a turtle and put it in the American's bed. When the American turned back the bed clothes he said, "What's this?"

"That's a Canadian bed bug," he replied. "Can you do any better than that?" — *Mahone Bay.*

Legend

The Payzant Legend

People in Mahone Bay, Lunenburg and Rose Bay tell the story of the Payzant tragedy and this is confirmed by Dr. H.A. Payzant, a descendant living in Dartmouth today. Louis Payzant was a Huguenot whose father had become a great ship builder in the Channel Isles. He liked to pioneer, and came to Canada with the founders of Halifax in 1749, arriving in one of his father's ships with materials for building a house. He did not remain in Halifax, but settled on Miesner's Island in Mahone Bay.

It is supposed that Mrs. Payzant was a sister of Montcalm, general of the French forces in Quebec, although later events seem to bear out the theory from other sources that she might have been an old sweetheart. At all events, Montcalm sent a band of Indians to take Marie and her family from their lonely island, and bring them to Quebec, and it was stipulated that there should be no bloodshed. When the Indians arrived at Mahone Bay they asked a boy to show them where the Payzants lived and then, in spite of their order, they tomahawked the boy for his scalp.

When Mr. Payzant heard the Indians' canoe grating upon the shore he took his gun and went out, having been told to use firearms if molested, and as soon as he realized the Indians were about to attack, he fired on them. They fired back and he fell. His wife came out when she heard the noise and he said, "Marie, my heart is failing."

He put his hand on the wound, which was bleeding freely, and then pressed it on a rock where the imprint still remains. At times it is seen clearly, a perfect impression of a man's hand with four fingers and a thumb, and tinged with the red of blood. At other times the imprint seems to fade away. It has been the subject of much speculation ever since, and so many tourists came later to see the stone that it was hauled away and locked up lest it be stolen.

There were several canoes full of Indians in the kidnapping party, and it must have been terrifying indeed when they rushed into the house. They scalped the nursemaid and the working man, looted the store, and set fire to the whole place. Then they took Marie and her three sons away, and as they went they could see their home burning. Mr. Payzant was left with his hand upon the rock and it is thought that the heat from the fire burned the imprint in indelibly. They say on Heckman's Island that the body was taken there for burial in a grove of trees, and that the grass beside the tree where he lies has always been green and remains green to this day. Some people also claim to have heard supernatural sounds.

The Indians then set out for Quebec, crossing by canoe to East River, through various waterways to the Ponhook Lakes, and down to the St. Croix. This river opens out at Windsor where there was a British fort, and at this point the Indians held tomahawks over Marie's head lest she alarm the sentry. Then they went down Avon River to the Basin of Minas, past Blomidon, through Minas Channel, and on to the Bay of Fundy. From there they went up St. John River to Woodstock. Here Marie's son, Louis, was threatened one day by a drunken Indian when he tried to take some blueberries the Indian had found, but fortunately the Indian fell in the river before he could carry out his threat and was drowned.

Mrs. Payzant expected a child, so she stopped at St. Anne's in Quebec where she was taken care of by nuns. The child's name was Lizette, but there is no further record of her so it is thought she might have been left with the nuns. The boys meanwhile were taken to Quebec where they were treated exceptionally well and given a good education. They were there for the Battle of Abraham and the fall of Quebec where Montcalm was fatally wounded. When he knew the end had come he asked to be taken to Marie and said, "I've brought a lot of trouble to you. I'm dying and I want you to forgive me."

Marie replied, "I'll forgive you, but not for the loss of my husband."

When the Payzants first came to Lunenburg they were offered a grant of land and, as often happened in those days, they occupied the land before the grant arrived. Marie was free now to return, and she petitioned the Governor in Council for her grant and it was made out to her. The grant provided certain obligations, but in spite of the fact that she was not supposed to sell her land she was given permission, which was most unusual. Naturally she did not wish to return to the scene of her husband's murder so, with true pioneer courage, she made a farm for herself and her sons at Falmouth, and here she was very successful. The family still have rough wooden kitchen chairs she made herself. One more item remains to be noted. Phillip one day saw the Indian who had murdered his father, so he shot him and fled to the States. The other sons remained with their mother and the name of Payzant has been prominen* in the province ever since. — *Dartmouth, Rose Bay, Lunenburg, Mahone Bay* and *Heckman's Island.*

Excerpts from
Bluenose
Ghosts

"I never expected to become a consultant on the supernatural," Helen Creighton commented, "but ever since *Bluenose Ghosts*, people phone to share their strange experiences with me; others will stop me in the supermarket to recount inexplicable happenings."

These people need reassurance from someone they feel would not laugh or make light of something which has made a profound impression upon them. Even now, scarcely a week goes by without such a phone call.

Bluenose Ghosts made its debut in 1957, one of the most memorable years in the author's life. She suddenly found herself in the limelight, from being the subject of a television documentary, to being requested to help plan and participate in a National Film Board production, *Songs of Nova Scotia*. In the middle of all this excitement she had to have unexpected surgery. Whilst still in hospital she was contacted by the president of Mount Allison University, asking her if she would accept an honorary degree and deliver the Convocation address. Six weeks later she did just that and experienced one of the happiest days of her life. It seemed strange at first to be addressed as "Dr." Creighton, but she soon stopped looking around for her physician brother!

The stories which appear in *Bluenose Ghosts* took nearly three decades to collect and came from almost every place she had visited in her search for folk songs; she had heard them from the beginning, when her first singers, the Hartlans, proudly told her of their "Ghost House." The Henneberrys on Devil's Island reported similar hauntings.

Bluenose Ghosts can be found in the Fiction section of the library, probably because some of the stories obviously originated in the imagination of the narrators, sprang from their fears or superstitious beliefs, or simply from an urge to spin a good yarn. Most accounts, however, are authentic, related by truly convinced people whose perceptions of life and death have been affected by a horrifying or heartening supernatural experience.

Bluenose Ghosts includes stories of pirates and buried treasure, phantom ships and crews, black dogs, ghostly rappings and footsteps, supernatural fires and lights, headless horses and men, white ladies and black witches; there are forerunners, poltergeists, dopplegangers, fairies, devils and angels. Some are terrifying, most are scary, but a few are uplifting spiritual experiences, offering glimpses of a blissful state of being. Helen Creighton listened and recorded them all; afterwards she often drove home alone over lonely country roads with a rapidly beating heart and chilled spine as moonlight and shadows combined to stir her already stimulated imagination. While acknowledging to herself that some of the stories could be discounted, there was a residue which seemed to echo her own experiences. The Three Death Knocks, for instance — she had twice heard them, with no visible being responsible, but they had been speedily followed by the death of someone close to her. She was often aware of guiding spirits which prompted her to take — or refrain from — some particular course. She believed that her Guardian Angel helped in times of need.

Whether *Bluenose Ghosts* is read for entertainment, an interest in folklore or the supernatural, the reader will find it impossible to put down, as the excerpts given here may demonstrate. This is Helen Creighton's best known book, a best seller with thirteen printings.

Forerunners

Forerunners are supernatural warnings of approaching events and are usually connected with impending death. They come in many forms, and are startling, as though the important thing is to get the hearer's attention. The most common forerunners are a picture falling off the wall or a calendar dropping to the floor at the moment when a distant loved one has died. Or you may hear your name called as I did when the mother of a friend died, although she had not called me at all. The three death knocks mentioned in the Prologue are forerunners and, to my knowledge, nobody has ever been able to explain them. Many people who disclaim any belief in ghosts admit to having had a forerunner which, after all, is just as much a part of the supernatural as the seeing of a spirit.

This is the widow's story . . .

"Father used to go to sea in the winters. When he left this time there were two little boys in our house. They were perfectly healthy and beautiful children. Mother didn't like staying in the house alone, so a cousin used to come and stay all night with her, and they slept together in the corner room. One night at twelve o'clock something woke them up and at first neither of them spoke. Finally my cousin said, 'Aunt Isabel, do you hear anything?' She said she did. It was a frosty night and what they heard was a rumbling coming down the road, rumble, rumble, rumble, rumble. It rumbled by the house like a wagon going over a frosty road. They were frozen in bed because it seemed to be coming straight towards our house, and that's what it did. It came rumbling around the house and stopped by the front door. They clung together in terror. Then they heard a knock like somebody pounding on something that was frozen. Then it sounded like something being thrown away. By and by it started again and turned around and rumbled back over the road until the sound was lost in the distance. They couldn't figure it out because they knew the sound of every wagon and who owned it, and who would that be driving up the road and turning off and stopping at their very door?

"They were up then, and they were afraid to go back to bed. Ma said, 'I'm going to get Maurice.' He was their neighbour, but Serena was afraid to go out. At the same time she wouldn't stay in the house alone, so both of them went and they woke Mr. Nickerson up and he came and stayed all night. He looked around but he couldn't see the track of any horse or wagon, so they thought it must be a forerunner and that my father was going to die. Ma cried and took on something awful, but the forerunner wasn't for my father. It was for one of the little boys who was taken sick and in a week was dead from diptheria.

"The day he was buried was frosty and cold, just as it had been that night. He had been prepared in the house for burial. Then the hearse started up the road for the funeral, and it made exactly the same noise they had heard. All the people in the house could hear it coming over the frosty ground, and it came rumbling up the frozen road and rumbled right up to the house. Then it stopped before the door just the way they heard it. Ma and my aunt couldn't speak. They were listening for the next thing to happen. The hearse had a door at the back with a lock, and the undertaker couldn't get the lock open, so he picked up a rock and hit it. Then he threw the rock away exactly as they'd heard it that night. Everything was repeated in detail and it happened about sixty years ago."

Another story came from a Mrs. McGillivray (Marion Bridge):

"Father was a builder and was working away from home, and mother was expecting him to finish his work and come back. She would not have been surprised if he came at any minute. One bright moonlight night she was sitting in her rocking chair with one ear cocked expectantly when she heard wagon wheels outside. Then everything was quiet until she heard him take the butt of the whip and give three strokes on the door, but he didn't come in. She went to the door to open it for him, supposing he might be carrying a load and didn't have a free hand, but there was no one there. She went out to the barn then, but the horse and wagon were not there, and apparently had not come into the yard at all. She was very alarmed then, thinking something must have happened to my father. Everybody knew what three knocks meant and nobody at the door when it was opened, so it was with a feeling of great relief that she heard his wagon wheels very soon afterwards, and saw him in the flesh as he appeared in his usual good health and spirits.

"My mother puzzled over this and wondered what it meant and later it was explained to her. At that time the body of a man was found up the Salmon River Road. The men who found it stopped at our house to change horses. They arrived at night, and at the very hour when she heard them before, and they came to the kitchen door and knocked with the butt of the whip three times. Everything was repeated."

Forerunners sometimes come as a kindly form of preparation where the shock of sudden death might be too great. An Amherst couple, for instance, lived happily together, and both were in excellent health. There was no reason to suppose any change would come to alter their unruffled lives. The house they lived in was very old and had bolts to fasten the doors. One night Rachel and her husband went to their room and he bolted the door as he always did. They were no sooner settled when she asked him to shut the door. He said, "I did." She said, "It's open," so he got up and closed it a second time. Once more they prepared themselves for sleep when again Rachel pointed out that the door was open. This time after closing it he got back in bed, but crawled in beside her and shivered and shook. She said, "What did you see?" but he refused to tell her. Finding him so greatly upset, and not being able to discover the reason, she appealed to her brother for help. "No," her husband said, "I won't tell you now, but if it ever comes to pass I'll tell you then." The next day Rachel took sick and a few days later she died and it was all very sudden and distressing. She was laid out in a white dress and, when her husband saw her like this, he said, "There, that's what I saw. Yes, I saw her laid out in her grave clothes."

At Liverpool Captain Godfrey's wife told me a strange story. "My husband was in his bunk ready to go to sea when first thing a bundle of papers came flying across the room and hit him. He thought his mate was having some fun, but he turned over and there was a blaze of fire the size of a man in the centre of the floor. A voice said, 'Don't go on this ship or you'll be lost. If you don't go you'll live to be an old man and you'll

47

die at home,' so he packed up and left the ship, but of course nobody knew why. They got a new captain and the ship sailed and was never heard of again. After that he sailed on ships all over the world and it was just as the voice said. When he died he was an old man and he died at home in his bed."

From Rev. Grant MacDonald (Dartmouth):

He had been born at Fourchu on the southern coast of the island. Not far from there the land jutted out into the sea and formed what was known as Winging Point. A man named Fred came to live there many years ago and settled in one of the small fishing shacks beside the water, but he could not remain there. Sounds came to disturb him, and these were so noisy that it was impossible for him to rest. He used to go to the nearest village and tell how he heard the voices of men shrieking as though in agony. His stories were not taken too seriously because he was an outsider and little was known of his background, but people encouraged him because he would be almost beside himself as he talked, and they were greatly entertained. Finally he could take it no longer and he moved away and nobody knew what became of him.

In former days there used to be many wrecks along this rocky shore, and in the spring of 1924 a trawler named *Mikado* foundered a few hundred yards from the place where he had lived. The sea was too rough for any of the crew to be rescued, and the people on shore looked helplessly on as sailors and all dropped one by one from the masts to which they were clinging, shrieking with despair. It was thought some may even have gone insane before they finally lost hold.

The fishing shack had been unoccupied for five years, ever since Fred had left it. Now it was opened up and, as soon as weather permitted, the bodies were brought in and placed upon the floor. As they were going about their sorry business the man recalled the sounds that Fred had reported. Ever since then the people roundabout have concluded that he had heard the forerunner of this event.

Leave 'em Lay

... from a fisherman at Spry Bay ...

"What I did see, brother Uriah and I. When my mother came to Mushaboom there was a place called Black de Cove and she dreamed there was money buried there. One foggy evening Uriah said to me, 'We're going to hunt for this money,' so he took a hoe and I took a shovel and we dug. The tide was low and we wasn't to speak to one another. After we got so far down we got a bone a foot long like a man's bone from the wrist to the elbow. The minute we got to it Uriah said, 'We're getting close to the money,' and I out the hole. You dassn't speak, you know, when you're digging for treasure. ... In five minutes the hole was full of water.

"Uriah should have thrown the bone back, but he didn't. He took it with him and, when we got home, he showed it to an old man we had in the house to teach school to the family. He was scared to death of it and told Uriah to take it back, but he didn't. That night it was dark and foggy and when he went out in the yard something chased him and it was as big as a puncheon. He claimed that after he went to bed he saw it come into the kitchen and he looked and saw it setting on a chair. He decided then that he wouldn't fool with it any longer and the next morning he took the bone and put it back in the hole. We never went digging again for the treasure, and the owner of the bone never troubled us any more."

Sometimes the stories take a ludicrous twist like this one from the Negro settlement of Preston.

"People passing the cemetery years ago were troubled by the appearance of the ghost of a man who was buried there. They decided he wanted a drink, so they got some rum, bored a hole through the ground to the coffin, and poured the rum down the hole. After that they were not afraid to pass the cemetery and they were never troubled again."

Mr. McMaster said — "They didn't get no rest at all, at all. They moved out as quick as they moved in. It was so bad that he twice hired a man to sleep there and see if they could discover what was wrong, for nothing had ever caused a disturbance in his father's day. In both cases when morning came he went to see what kind of a night they had put in, he found that a man was dead. He offered a large amount of money then to anybody who would sleep in that house and about that time a soldier came along.

"That feller, the soldier, went in and stayed all night. He heard a little noise about eleven o'clock at night from the other side of the house and there was a skeleton come down and he started playing around on the floor. He watched him for a while, but he got tired of looking at him and he walked down to the other end of the house and went to bed, leaving the skeleton rolling around the floor. The next morning the son who owned the house but couldn't live in it came to see if the soldier was still alive. When he saw that he was living, he said, 'What did you see last night?'

" 'I didn't see nothing or hear nothing that would scare me,' he said. 'I want to stay here for a couple more nights before I have anything I can tell you.'

"The second night was pretty much the same as the first but, on the third night when the skeleton was dancing and tearing around, the soldier said, 'What in the name of God kind of man are you?' So the skeleton said, 'I'm glad you spoke to me like that. I wouldn't touch you. I didn't touch the other fellows who were here but they got frightened. I could tell the first time I seen you that I could get you to speak. (Many people think the ghost can speak if the human opens the conversation.) You're not a coward at all!'

"Then he told him that he was the man who had owned the place, and that his son was scared his funeral would cost him money, so he hadn't buried him right. He'd made a cheap funeral. He said, 'You talk to my son and tell him to dig into the graveyard and take my remains up and make a wake for me and notify all the neighbours around. Then when he notifies all the neighbours he is to make a good funeral for me and, if he does that, no one will hear nothing from me any more.' So the son did as his father wished and the family lived peacefully in the house forever after."

At Berwick the story is told of a family who came to the eastern end of the Province soon after the Acadians left. They

50

hired a yoke of oxen and a French plough from a neighbour. They were brought up with a jerk as the plough caught in the bail a huge iron pot. The farmer suddenly realized what it was and sat on the ground to hide it. He said to the boy working with him, "Unhook the oxen and take them home. You can leave the plough where it is. I have a violent cramp in my stomach and when I recover I'll let you know." As soon as the boy left he unearthed the pot and with its contents, he and his wife bought a fine house. When they died they left a property worth $12,000. The pot was about two feet across and was kept in the family for many years. The story was told to me by the descendants. Other French money was supposed to have been found on Goat Island by men named Delap and Holliday.

Ghosts Guard Buried Treasure

From a Micmac Indian:

There used to be pirates around on the south shore of Nova Scotia and one day this Indian named Glode was out in his canoe, he had his little girl with him and when they got to a place where there is a point of land, he saw a ship sailing towards them. They were scared of strangers in those days, so he paddled into a cove and hid his canoe away in the woods. Then he climbed a tree. From there he could see everything that went on, and he watched that ship. It stopped and the pirates on board took down the sails, lowered a rowboat and four or five of them came ashore. They came straight to that point, chose a spot and started digging. The captain gave the orders. After they got a trench dug big enough, he sent two of the men to the boat for a big chest. After they had brought it up and put it down beside the hole he lined them all up and said, "Have you got everything ready? Who's going to keep this money?" One of them says, 'Well, the other fellows don't say much. I'll look after it.'

" 'All right,' said the captain, 'you're to guard it for a hundred and fifty years,' and before the man realized what he had got himself into, the others grabbed him. They cut off his head and then they put him in the hole with the chest. After that they drew a map, covered up the hole, and went away.

"When the ship was out of sight Glode came down from the tree. He didn't know what the dead man was supposed to do, so he wasn't afraid to dig him up. He wanted to see what was in that chest. It was mostly gold. In those times Indians used to wear a sort of gown with no sleeves, so he took that off and piled in all that he could carry. Then he covered the place up again and got his little girl and the canoe. As they paddled towards the open water he got thinking that it wasn't safe for an Indian to have money and he'd be better off without it. By this time he had reached a great big ledge two or three feet wide, and he'd made up his mind. He poured that money down in the split of the rock, and he never went back for it. For all I know, that money is there yet."

Mr. Enos Hartlan of South East Passage had been the first to tell me about the pirates' custom, but he varied his story at one point. He said that when the man volunteered to stay with the treasure "They had a party and they soused him (made him drunk) and buried him alive with the treasure."

At East Petpeswick a man named Stingles lived to tell of his narrow escape in one of these episodes. He was new to pirates' ways and was just about to offer, "but a darkie said it first and they off his head an' fired him down the hole." And at Port Hastings a story has been handed down, through three generations, of a woman who was in the barn when she saw a coloured man running down over the hill. He told men in the village that he had heard the pirates planning to kill him and bury him with a treasure and he had made his escape. He told them they had killed another coloured man the day before.

The burial of a human being with the treasure has led to many strange beliefs and there are countless stories of his obedience to his orders. Whether he ever actually functioned as a guardian is an open question, but the fact that he might do so had an extraordinary psychological effect. Many a time a group of men have got as far as finding the chest, and one of them has spoken, thus breaking an inviolable rule. Without waiting to see what would happen they have simply dropped their shovels and fled, confident that the whole expedition was ruined by the indiscretion of one spoken word. For with

52

human speech the guardian ghost was given power which, until then, it could not use. After the power was released, anything could happen, and if our tales are to be believed, things often did.

Mr. Horace Johnston, farmer and fisherman of Port Wade, used to say, "Sometimes I tell the truth and sometimes I don't." This is supposed to be one of his true stories (I think).

"When I was a young man a Scotsman came here and claimed his father had sailed with Kidd. He had a chart and he supposed Kidd had hid his treasure at Hudson's Point. Four of us went with him to dig but, for all I know, the treasure is there yet. I saw the chart and I went once to find it, but I'll never go again.

"These treasures are supposed to be dug at night, so we went at ten o'clock. We could tell exactly where it was by the chart. In those days when the treasure would have been buried a man was killed and buried with it to stand guard. The Scotsman had hunted up some pretty brave fellows to help him and he was a-digging on even shares. I was young then and I didn't fear the devil or anyone else. If he came along and I couldn't cope with him I figgered I could run. We had a man named Corneil, Ike Fleet, the Scotsman, and me. That made four.

"Well sir, we hadn't been digging long before we had an extra man with us. We had five, and he was there all night. While we was a-digging in the hole with pick and shovel and throwing stones, we didn't notice the fifth man but, when one of the party crawled up out of the hole and looked back, there were still four below. He dassn't speak, but beckoned us up, all but this extry man. Then we went away and talked it over.

"Who's the fifth man?" he says. We went back and there he was all alone in the hole now and still digging. All at once there was the devilishest noise I ever heard. The ground trembled and the rocks shook. I began to get tender-footed and the rest were shaking, but we had one brave man among us. That was Ike Fleet, when it got too tough for us and we mentioned leaving, Ike said, "No, I'm not going to leave. We've come to dig a treasure. We heard a little noise, but that's thunder. Maybe it was the extra man digging deeper and rolling a big stone that made a noise like thunder. Anyhow, I'm going back," and mind you, he did. It took a brave man to do that, and a foolish one. We were twenty feet from the shore, and the tide was a hundred feet out as it often gets in the Annapolis Basin. First thing we knew Ike was in the waters of the Basin to his neck, and none of us knew how he got there. He wasn't hurt, but we didn't have any trouble getting him home after that.

"What did this extry man look like? He looked like any of the rest of us working at night. He was a medium height and he was digging with pick and shovel just like we were doing. Whether he really put Ike in the Annapolis Basin or not I don't know but, if he didn't, how did he get there all of a sudden, 120 feet away? I'd like to know the answer to that, but I'm not going back to find out."

Foresight and Hindsight

Told by Mr. Alex Morrison, son of the blacksmith . . .

"A strange thing happened just before Sandy Munro fell over the bridge and got drowned. At that time Neil McPherson was just a lad and he was walking over the Marion Bridge one night with his mother. He stopped for a moment and said, 'Come here mother and look at the little boy lying on the bottom of the river.' His mother couldn't see anything and told him to come along home. It was just after this that Sandy was drowned, but that wasn't all that happened.

"About that time they were seeing a light on a boat up the river at Grand Mira. The owner wanted to sell the boat but nobody would buy it, being suspicious that something might be wrong with it on account of the light. My father wanted it, light or not, so he bought it.

"They always thought foul play had caused Sandy's death. The night before he died the irons in the smith were making a great racket. You could hear them in the forge and they seemed to be jumping around. Sandy and the blacksmith were friends and the boy often did errands for him. Just before he died the blacksmith had asked him to take an axe across the bridge for him. He was doing this when he must have met two boys who were known to be bad and whose mother was said to be a witch. Someone saw the boys having a tussle on the bridge and, a while later, the body was discovered lying in the water as Neil McPherson had described him to his mother.

"They called on the blacksmith then to get the boy. The grappling irons he used to take him from the water were the ones that had jumped in the forge the night before, and the boat that he took to go out on the river was the one that had shown the strange lights and that nobody would buy but my father. After the body was recovered Sandy's mother had a dream. She thought the boy came to her and pointed to the blacksmith's axe as it stood in its place at the forge, and said, 'That's the axe that killed me.' And when Sandy's body was laid out on the bridge of the boat my father had bought, there was a lot of people from the village who came to look at him. One was the boy who was supposed to have murdered him. You know it's an old belief if a murderer passes by or touches the person he has murdered, that blood will issue from the wound, and that is exactly what happened. The wound that killed Sandy was in his temple and, as the suspected murderer walked past him, blood flowed from the wound and stopped as soon as he went by. The thing was hushed up and the boys and their mother moved away, but that's the way it all happened."

At Port Hood I talked to two women who had one day seen a city and two churches on a site where there was a later drilling for oil. To date that city has not transpired, but it is expected to come some day. Train headlights were seen long before there was any train. At Wellington, Prince Edward Island, in December, 1885, a phantom train was seen by forty people. Two extraordinary stories were confided to me in the summer of 1956 . . .

"My husband had multiple sclerosis. He has always been a good-living man but has never been particularly religious. He is well educated but not an intellectual. The doctors thought an operation might help him and he was sent to Montreal. He has always been perfectly clear in his mind. He only once mentioned what happened and has never referred to it again. I respect his silence because it must be a wonderfully precious memory. He said that one night Christ came and sat upon his bed. No word was spoken, but he felt a deep peace."

"When Rev. Mr. Hares was in Windsor I attended a Whitsunday celebration of holy communion in the Anglican church. He was a deeply spiritual man. As he was preparing the elements I looked up and was startled to see a brilliant tongue of flame that rested for a brief period on the top of his head and then vanished. It did not move nor flutter, but lay flat, just as it must have done on the heads of the disciples. I watched in fear and my knees trembled. Then I looked to see what the other parishioners were making of it but I realized they hadn't observed it. The vision seemed to be for my eyes alone and I was greatly upset. For a long while I kept it to myself, then finally told Mr. Hares. He was most disturbed. We discussed it and agreed it couldn't have been a shaft of light through a stained glass window, nor was there anything else to explain it. This took place about a year before he died."

"At that time accommodation was hard to find in Halifax, but it was necessary for me to spent a few nights there. I had a friend who was living in an apartment on Barrington Street . . . They occupied three small rooms on the ground floor that opened out from each other and were in a row. Frances and Alex slept in one room and I slept with their child in a bed that was placed so that my head was close to the wall nearest them. There was nothing between but a thin partition. A gentle tapping on the wall from my side would have awakened them. It was poor accommodation, but the best they could get at that time.

"I must have been asleep for some hours when I was wakened by the sound of bottles clinking, knives slashing, and men talking, and they were right there in the room with me. I was terrified, but, after a little while, I forced myself to open one eye to see what was happening. To my surprise I saw four men sitting around a card table. I only looked long enough to get a vivid picture of one of them. He was probably the leader. I can see him plainly today. He was a big man with an oily look about his face, and he had a dark moustache. He was a swarthy man. One thing that I distinctly noticed was either a bright red kerchief that he was wearing, or it might have been the sleeve of his shirt. He held a long knife in his hand and the blade was silver. It was the sound of cards and the whisky bottles that woke me up.

"I saw all this in one quick look. Then I closed my eyes and lay there, paralysed with fright for the rest of the night. I was even too frightened to call my friends or knock on the wall to wake them up. When daybreak came the noise stopped, and I still didn't open my eyes until my friend's husband came through my room on his way to work. I kept saying to myself, 'You're not asleep, you're awake. It isn't a dream.' When Alex went through I looked up. Men, tables and bottles were all gone, and there was nothing in the room that hadn't been there when I went to sleep and there was no sign of any disturbance . . . After I got away I went to see another friend and there told what I had seen. The friend knew the place well and said it had been a hotel at one time with a window that opened out on an alleyway. At that time the apartment was all one room. One man would take it and let others in through the window and they would drink and play cards. At one time, he said, a lad of sixteen was stabbed there . . . I must have looked back on an event that took place perhaps a hundred or more years before."

Devils and Angels

According to a story from Middle Musquodoboit, Ike Foley was responsible for his own death, although he did not anticipate it when he spoke. "He was an awful man to swear. There was a hussock, a rock in the stream that bothered them when they were river-driving. He got mad and said if the devil would come he would go out and help him, and together they would take the rock out of that stream. The boys laughed at him and said if the devil's voice came he'd be too scared to go out, but that evening they heard it. Ike wouldn't go, but they all got after him and dared him, not thinking it was really the devil they heard. It came three times, but still Ike wouldn't go. Next morning when they went out the rock was gone, and nobody knew who moved it. Shortly after that, Ike was walking on thin ice at the place and he fell through and got drowned. We always felt the devil got him and, after that, you could hear the devil's chains rattling whenever you went by."

Many years ago several little children were lost in the woods near Sambro and they had to sleep out all night in the dark. Their parents and friends were nearly frantic as they thought of the terrors that would beset them. The shore is very rocky here and the waves pounding in the darkness would frighten much older and stouter hearts. Imagine the astonishment of the searchers then when they found the children looking perfectly happy and untroubled. Afraid? They looked surprised at such a question. Why would they be afraid? They were all right, they said, because an angel had sat up with them all night.

Phantom Ships and Sea Mysteries

Occasionally a single ghost turns up on a ship. This story from Glen Haven . . . Ben Smeltzer was a West Dover man and one of the crew of a vessel fishing off Georges in winter. It was snowing and there were no fish, and they were getting all iced up and the captain had decided to take the ship to Boston. At this time Mr. Smeltzer went down below and, when he went into the cabin, there was a strange man sitting at the chart table writing on a slate — a large, healthy-looking seafaring man.

For readers who are not accustomed to the sea and its ways, I might mention that it would be impossible in the limited space of a sailing vessel for a person to stow away for any length of time, if at all, and this vessel had been at sea for some weeks.

"Who can this be?" Mr. Smeltzer thought. "What does it mean?" He had heard of strange events at sea, and he scratched his head as he went up the companionway to talk it over with his captain.

"There's a strange man down below," he said. "Never see him before."

"You're crazy," said the captain. Then observing that Mr. Smeltzer was serious about it he decided to humour him and added in a voice that had in it more than a hint of sarcasm, "What did you say to him?"

"I didn't say anything," Mr. Smeltzer declared. "He can't be human."

"Well," said the captain, who began to have misgivings himself, "you come down with me and show me your man." So down they went and there was no one there. However the captain was a thorough man and Mr. Smeltzer had stated specifically that the stranger had been sitting at the chart table writing on a slate. He therefore strode over to the table and picked up the slate. The top side was clean, just as he had left it. Without really thinking what he was doing he turned the slate over and there he was amazed to see a message. It read: "Change your course to nor' nor' west and steer so many hours and you'll come to a vessel turned on its side and the crew hanging to it."

He put the slate down and snorted.

"Tricks. Sailors must always be at their tricks," but Mr. Smeltzer insisted it was not a trick and he grew even more serious as he too read the message. More to satisfy him than anything, the captain called his crew down one by one and had each write something on the slate. No script resembled the mysterious handwriting. By this time the crew all knew the story and they were as one in concluding they should follow the slate's directions. Against his own wishes and judgment the captain changed his course. And sure enough, they had not gone far on their way when they came upon an upturned vessel. Men were still clinging to the hull, and they were in time to save them. They supposed then that the stranger who had appeared in the cabin had been one of the first to succumb and that he had taken this means of saving his fellow seamen.

. . . according to Mr. Enos Roast of East Chezzetcook. "It must have happened sixty years ago that an iron vessel was found outside Halifax with nobody on board, but with the table set for breakfast. This looked as though it had been abandoned hastily. The vessel belonged to Liverpool, England, but people were suspicious of her and nobody wanted to take her back to her owners. Finally Captain Sprott Balcolm of Salmon River said he would. After they got out of the harbour one of the crew, Jack Donaldson, said to him, 'We've got a good thing here.' 'How's that?' and he told of finding a long chest. He said, 'There might be something in that chest.' The captain was curious then and went with Donaldson to see it. They stood talking about it and wondering what might be inside and, after a while, they decided to open it. It wasn't locked, so all they had to do was lift the cover. They did this and, right on top, was a lady's watch. The rest of the chest was filled with her beautiful clothes.

"The captain wrote it all down in his log and nineteen days later when they landed in Liverpool, an investigation was held. The watch and clothing were used as evidence, and it was supposed that the lady had been murdered." But why had the captain and the crew left the ship, and what had become of them? It must have been something extraordinary that would force them to abandon their ship, and so close to a large seaport. Mr. Roast could not answer that question, but in time the words of some of the old folk songs came to mind, and with them a possible solution. For in these songs it is not uncommon for a person who has been murdered to return and take revenge.

With all the people I have talked to, I have only two reports of sea serpents . . . Cranberry Lake lies roughly in the Sydney area. It is about a mile in length and is always full of water. One evening about thirty years ago a man was standing by the lake, looking for cows that had strayed away, when he was astonished to see something move on the surface that looked like a horse's head. Then the neck appeared. In a moment the animal or sea serpent went under water, turning itself over so that the last he saw of it was its tail. He judged it to be twelve feet in length and it seemed to be looking for something on the shore. It all happened so quickly that he could not recall any other details. Others have also told of seeing it, and stories have been current for one hundred years.

As recently as six years ago a man went to the lake to wash his car and, as he was working, it appeared again. He was so frightened that he gathered his things together and fled. Shortly after this a company was formed to go to the lake and find and kill the animal. It was winter and they had to work through the ice, but they were unable to find it. Some say it is all a myth; others insist they too have seen it.

Ghosts Helpful, Harmful and Headless

Of all the ghost stories I have heard, I know of none so comforting and touching as this from a man in Dartmouth . . .

"When I was a young man I was out courting and I had to come home over a lonely road that had very few houses. It was a bright moonlight night. Before long I heard footsteps and noticed a shadow behind me. I walked a little faster, and so did the person following me. Then I slowed down, and so did he. When I got to within about two hundred yards from the house I turned around to see who it was and there, standing in the road was my father who had been dead for nearly three years. I saw him clearly, even to the gold watch and chain that he always wore, and that I always connected with him in my thoughts. I was too frightened to speak, but ran in the house and got into bed and under the clothes where I lay shaking for the rest of the night.

"In the morning I got up and went to work, and there I was told a very strange thing. There were three men who thought I had done something that I hadn't, and they had been hiding in the bushes as I walked home, planning to attack me. When they saw another man walking along behind me they didn't dare, and so I suppose my life was saved. It is many years since this happened, but it is as vivid today as it was the night it occurred."

So Many Wandering Women

Dr. Robinson of Annapolis Royal used to hear the story of the Grey Lady and, if my memory serves me faithfully, it was from his family that I learned of his meeting with her. It happened one night when he was driving home from a call. He came to an elbow in the road where there was a small bridge that crossed a brook, and there were alder thickets that grew close to the side of the road. As he drew near the bridge his horse stopped. He got out of his old-fashioned gig with its big spider wheels and went to the horse's head. There he saw the Grey Lady standing in front of the horse and trying to stop him. As he approached she disappeared from sight. The horse was so agitated that he took it by the bridle and led it along. When they got to the bridge he discovered that it had been washed out by a spring freshet and, if he had not been stopped in this extraordinary way, he would probably have had a bad accident. He recalled then that other people had told of seeing her on this bridge, and that her appearance was usually a warning of one kind or another. This was a foggy night when he would not have been able to see the gap until too late.

A story from England;
"Rev. Mr. Gray belonged to a large family and had been recently ordained. This was in the early Edwardian period. He had taken a parish in the East End of London. His housekeeper had gone to bed and he was sitting in his study smoking his pipe and thinking out his sermon for Sunday. Presently the door bell — a spring bell — rang and he went to answer it. Standing under the gas light in the fog stood a little old lady in poke bonnet and shawl and a once black skirt now green with age. She pleaded with him to go to an address in the West End of London. She said he must go because he was urgently needed. The young clergyman tried to put her off as it was very late, but she pleaded so earnestly that he finally promised to go that same night.

"He took a cab and at length arrived at the address. It turned out to be one of the large mansions in the West End and it was lit up and obviously there was a party going on. After he had rung the bell and waited, the butler came and the clergyman said, 'I believe I'm wanted here. My name is Gray.'

"The butler said, 'Have you an invitation?'

" ' No, but I've been asked to come. Some one needs me.'

The butler asked him to wait in the little anteroom and presently brought back the master of the house. He was a well-known titled gentleman. Mr. Gray then told him what had happened and the man looked very odd and asked if he could describe his visitor. As he did so the man looked terrified. He then confessed to having led a wicked life of crime which included white slavery, whereupon the clergyman tried to help him. He urged him to stop this life and make his peace with God, and the man finally made what appeared to be a serious confession. The clergyman then gave him absolution and said in leaving, 'Just to show you're in earnest, I'll be celebrating holy communion at eight-thirty in the morning and I want you to be there.' Then he went away.

"The next morning as the priest turned to administer the sacrament it was obvious that the man was not there and he wondered what he should do about it. After breakfast he decided he should see him again. He arrived at the mansion house, now still and quiet, and at his ring, the butler came. When he asked to see his master the butler told him he was dead. Mr. Gray said, 'It can't be true. I was talking to him last night.'

" 'Yes I know. I recognize you,' the butler said. 'He died shortly after you left.'

"Mr. Gray asked if he could see the body which he knew must still be in the house, and the butler took him up to a very spacious room. There, lying on the bed, was the dead body of the man he'd been talking to the night before. He stood for a moment thinking, trying to puzzle it out and, as he did so, he glanced around the room. His eye caught an oil painting above the bed. It was of a little old lady in a poke bonnet and shawl — the same little old lady who had come to him and had sent him to this house. He said to the butler,

" 'Who is the little old lady?'

" 'That is the master's mother. She died many years ago.' "

Another pleasant story of a helpful ghost comes from New Brunswick.

"I was fishing with me father way back of Shippigan and that night a big storm come and we had a very small vessel, about thirty feet long and three sail on it. We were not coming very fast but we got lost and we couldn't see the Tracadie light. We looked and there was a woman dressed in white and a torch in her hand and her two feet dragging, and she was canted this way." (Here he held his hand up to show that she was not standing upright, but at a slant.) "Me father took the wheel then and he followed her for twenty minutes and then she disappeared and, as she went out of sight, the Tracadie lights came into view. I was about fifteen years old then. I'm eighty-eight now, but I never forgot that. I don't know who she was, but I guess she saved our lives all right."

A woman at Clarks Harbour told a strange story.

"There is a big rock at Centreville Woods called the Ghost Rock. When my mother was a girl about fifteen she was at Centreville visiting her sister. When she decided one night to go home, my uncle said he would go with her rather than have her go through the woods alone. They were walking along without saying very much when all of a sudden they saw something white crossing the road ahead of them, over and back.

"Did you see what I saw?" my uncle said.

"Well, I saw something white crossing the road," she said. They walked on a little further and it came again in front of them across the road, and it looked like a woman dressed in a white gown and the tail of it was long and sweeping and trailed along behind her.

"You can keep on going to Stony Island or come back with me, but I'm not going any further," my uncle said. My mother decided to keep going and, just as he was turning back, she saw it in front of her again and from then she knew nothing until she lifted the latch of her own front door. When she told what had taken place her mother asked her why she hadn't stopped at her brother's store, but she had no recollection of having passed any store. It was as though she had been picked up and carried home. It was not until the parcel she was carrying fell to the ground and startled her as she touched the latch that she was conscious of her surroundings."

There and Not There

Another story from Cape Breton was given to me by Mrs. Ruth Metcalfe. "A young couple in their thirties lived at Reserve Mines. She was a tall and lovely lady of highland Scottish birth. He was a miner named John McNeil. In those days it was the custom for cows to be pastured on common land and one summer afternoon Mrs. McNeil started out to bring their cow home. She was dressed in a beautiful black silk dress with a white apron which was the usual costume for that class of highland woman. She had not gone far when she met a neighbour and they walked together, enjoying the early afternoon sunshine as old friends do who have met unexpectedly. Their conversation was interrupted by Mrs. McNeil who said with surprise, 'There's John. I'll go for the cow later,' and she left to go to her home and husband.

" 'I'm going for my cow, so I'll bring yours home too, Lizzie,' her neighbour said, and she did.

"When the neighbour came back with the two cows she stopped first at her own home, and was surprised to see her husband there, for he was not expected for some time.

" 'Why are you home so early?' she said.

" 'John McNeil was killed in the mine this afternoon,' he replied. When she recovered from the shock she asked the time of the accident, remembering how his wife had looked towards her house and how surprised she had been to see her husband there. She realized then of course that he had appeared at the moment of his death."

Fairies

I had often inquired for fairies but, until then, it seemed that they had not crossed the water from the old land. This was the exception.

"When we were children we lived in a house at Point Edward. There were six of us sleeping upstairs. The upper part of the house wasn't finished off and there were rafters above that could be seen from both of the bedrooms where we were sleeping. This morning we were lying in bed and we looked up and we could see a dozen little people like pixies or elves with brownish bodies jumping back and forth on the beams, carrying on and having a time of it. I can't remember their clothes, but they were about a foot high and wore high pointed caps and shoes. I called my sisters and they were watching the same thing. It happened only once, and it lasted for about ten minutes. Then they vanished and were never seen again. With all their jumping round they didn't make a sound."

Haunted Houses and Poltergeists

In the days when Devil's Island had some fifty inhabitants there was one house that was noted for the extraordinary things that happened in it. This treeless little island at the mouth of Halifax Harbour, one mile in circumference, was then a thriving fishing community. Small boats were used and men would fish singly or with a companion. The Atlantic Ocean was at their door, so they did not have far to go.

One day when Henry Henneberry was out, his wife heard him return and walk into the kitchen. The flopping of his rubber boots was a familiar sound. At that particular moment, as she heard him moving noisily about, he was drowned. In his absence she had been painting the floor, and his footsteps appeared in the fresh paint. She had also washed a mat that morning and had left it lying on another floor and his footprint was plainly outlined here as well.

Fires used to occur in this house in a mysterious manner. You could put your hand on the shingles and they would not be hot even though you could see the fire burning. All the people who have lived in the house have been Roman Catholics, and they always put palm in the rafters for protection. This palm, blessed in the church and given out on Palm Sunday, would never be touched, even though the fire would burn all around it. Different families lived in the house, and they all had the same experience. One man described the fires as five or six blue blazes that were not "natural" fires. One family insisted that the house collapsed on them one night and

66

that they got out of bed and said their rosaries after which the house went back to its proper shape again. They even tried putting the house on a different foundation but it still caught fire, this time under the roof. Here, with no water supply except from wells, it would be a major calamity to have a house catch fire because it would be almost impossible to put it out, so this is further proof that the fires had some strange unexplainable quality.

"When I grow up I want to write a book. If I could write just one book I'd be so happy." Helen Creighton as a graduate of the Halifax Ladies' College.

"When you're young life's full of adventure," Dr. Creighton remin-
isces. *In 1920 she drove this Red Cross van across Nova Scotia, taking medical services to remote areas of the province.*

Helen Creighton Collection, P.A.N.S.

TOP RIGHT:
Devil's Island is about one mile in circumference and lies just off
Eastern Passage at the mouth of Halifax Harbor. Now uninhabited,
the island was once a thriving fishing community and home to some
50 people, including the Henneberrys.

Helen Creighton Collection, P.A.N.S. Photographer: Bill Mont

RIGHT:
Children of Devil's Island helping Helen Creighton with her
melodeon which she moved in a wheelbarrow.

Helen Creighton Collection, P.A.N.S.

Ben Henneberry

Helen Creighton capturing on tape the Gallagher family of Chebucto Head. The family was the source of many songs, including the version of The Broken Ring Song printed in this book, as sung by Mrs. Edward Gallagher.

Helen Creighton with Clary Croft and Mary Sparling.

William Riley of Cherry Brook first sung "The Cherry Tree Carol" for Dr. Creighton. At the time he was 86 years old, blind and deaf. He was a very religious man and sang with great feeling, especially those songs which spoke of the bliss of the heavenly home.

A lifetime highlight — On Nov. 20, 1987 a tribute to Canada's First Lady of Folklore was performed in Halifax, when a choice selection of her folk songs was performed by Symphony N.S. under conductor Dr. Walter Kemp, featuring the Dalhousie Chorale, Mary Kelly and Clary Croft. Pictured here are, L-R, Dr. Kemp, Mary Kelly, Scott MacMillan, arranger, Dr. Creighton and Clary Croft.

Photographer: George Georgakakos

Excerpts from
Bluenose
Magic

Bluenose Magic, Popular Beliefs and Superstitions in Nova Scotia, was first published in 1968. A decade later it was produced in a paperback edition. This book is a natural sequel to *The Folklore of Lunenburg County, N.S.*, since a large percentage of the material was collected in the same area and deals with similar subjects, although there may be a greater emphasis on witchcraft and enchantment, superstitions and home remedies.

The material for this book was collected under the auspices of the National Museum of Canada, which employed Helen Creighton for twenty years. At this time her attention was drawn to the fact that a huge dictionary of *Popular Beliefs and Superstitions* was being compiled, with material being sought all over the continent. She was considered the obvious person to contribute the section on Nova Scotian folklore. The Director of the National Museum and the head of the Folklore Section gave this project their blessing with the result that Helen began extracting material from her bulging files as the basis of *Bluenose Magic*.

Nova Scotia's settlers included English, French, Scotch (a word Helen preferred to Scottish), Irish, German and Negroes, in addition to the indigenous Micmac Indians (now a minority). Consequently she collected material from all these ethnic groups, continually being surprised to note that similar beliefs, remedies or superstitions cropped up without regard to the racial background of the informant. It would be a challenge to scholars engaged in tracing the origins of popular beliefs — whether there was a common background to be discovered in the distant past, or were the different groups forced to the same conclusions by their observations and experience?

The large section on witchcraft and enchantment emphasizes the important part these beliefs played in the lives of our forebears. At a time before television and radio, before the telephone and automobile, before the advent of electricity, when winter meant long months of isolation in small communities, neighbours were of utmost importance; their habits and idiosyncrasies came under close scrutiny. Eccentric behavior would be marked and commented upon, losing nothing in the telling, would even be embroidered by the superstitious, the fearful, or the spiteful. Thus it would not be difficult to gain a reputation for being weird — a witch, even. Some would have enjoyed the power implied by such a reputation. So witches there were, of both sexes, able to weave a spell or an enchantment, to bewitch cattle or children. And there were people who knew how to break spells, lift curses, foil the witch. Perhaps today such beliefs would be regarded with amusement, but when Helen Creighton collected the stories fifty years ago many people took these things seriously with frequent references to witches in the Bible. They used sacred words and symbols for their protection, as well as mundane things such as a broomstick laid across the doorstep or a dogwood cross nailed above the door, a horseshoe hung over the entrance to the barn.

Almost any reader would find *Bluenose Magic* fascinating, especially those interested in the region and its folklore. Scholars would find it invaluable, both for its content and the organization of the material. Each item is numbered and the ethnic origin and location of every informant given. There are copious footnotes and cross-references; it is fully indexed and a bibliography is supplied for those wishing to delve deeper into the subject.

The Supernatural

Perhaps Nova Scotians are particularly sensitive to supernatural experiences because we are a sea-faring people or, if not, at least we have the sea all around us. Material has always come easily but now, since *Bluenose Ghosts* appeared in 1957, it has been astonishing how many people tell of experiences they wish to share, but they must be sure they have a sympathetic ear. Heretofore they feared the scoffer who would laugh and say they only imagined the event, for nothing is more frustrating to the person who has experienced the unexplainable ... These things are pondered and discussed in the academic parlour and by fishermen as they mend their nets, for the supernatural is no respecter of persons.

Visions

My name is Colin Francis McFarlane, and this man was Colin Francis McKinnon, first cousin to Bishop McKinnon. He was a very religious man and my godfather, and lived to be ninety-seven years old. He told many times how at midnight mass the old people in the old days had to walk four miles to the church. This Christmas night was blustery. He and his wife, Angus Rory McDonald, and another McDonald couple started to walk, leaving at 10:30. The trestle bridge below the station was in such darkness that they were afraid to go across. They stood there for ten minutes wondering what to do, when to their astonishment a bright light shone on the bridge and the six of them were able to go across. It looked like a great big star and was so bright that it lit up the bridge, and that bridge was one thousand feet long.

    This was a dangerous bridge to cross if you couldn't see your way, and dangerous any time if a train came and you couldn't get off in time. They were following the railway because it was clear of snow and made good walking. There was not a train in the place less than three hours before or after the event.

I heard the story from all six who had crossed the bridge that night, and Mrs. McKinnon always told it on Christmas night. They couldn't tell exactly where the light was from, but they thought it showed for a hundred feet. It was spitting snow and blowing and the light was so strong they only knew it was right over the bridge and lit up long enough for them to get to the other side. (Antigonish, Scotch)

Witchcraft

We seldom use the word *hex* in Nova Scotia. A person goes out witching, and one is witched or bewitched. The word witch is applied to male or female without distinction. Magic counter-charms known as charms are used widely in both witchcraft and cures where the person is supposed to be the victim of magic or the evil eye.

Characteristics of Witches

A woman told of a witch trying to teach her to be a witch. She used to come here from Dover and stay. The witch liked her and asked her if she'd like to learn to bewitch people and have fun. She got to telling her what she'd have to do. She had to sign a lease of her life to the devil, curse her father and mother, cut her finger and sign her name in the blood. That was enough and she wouldn't go any further. She was sixteen at the time and had thought it would be fun to go through a keyhole. (Seabright, German, Scotch and English)

A Witch Foiled

The wife of Daddy Red Cap, the wizard, had a friend visiting her from Black Point. She told this friend that she could teach her the Black Art and then she could put a spell on anyone she

72

wanted to. She said, "You must say certain things like, 'and I sell my soul to the devil.' "

The friend wouldn't say that, but said instead, "I'll sell my soul to the Lord."

A terrible commotion followed and the wife said, "You've ruined me, you've ruined me, you've ruined me," and the friend was frightened then and ran away. (Allandale, English, Irish and Scotch)

A witch can't get over a broomstick until the sun goes down. Old Mother N. was at a house and she kept saying, "I want to go home," but a broomstick was across the door and she had to wait until the sun went down. (French Village, English and French)

If you put the broom across the door, the witches can't cross. If you see somebody coming that's a witch, you put the broom down and they won't come over it. They won't come in; they'll come to the door and they'll go home again. (Rose Bay, German)

Bessie was supposed to be a witch. She went into a house one time and said, "I knew what they were doing. They'd boiled new pins in milk and then put them under a cushion, but I sat right down on them." If she had been a witch the pins would have jumped up. (Port Medway, New England)

Disposal of Witches

Here they have a charm using needles and pins which force the witch to come and beg for relief. They also believe a witch can't step over a broomstick, and that if they place a pair of scissors or a knife over the threshold and the witch steps over it, her spirit will be weakened. (Preston, Negro)

Years ago a Negro in Preston went in his barn and found his horse wet and foaming at the mouth as though it had been ridden hard. He decided it had been witch ridden, so he went to the store and got ten new needles and ten new pins and put them in a bottle. Then he went out on a lake (the ocean would serve the same purpose) filled the bottle with water so it would sink, and then dropped the bottle in the lake. After that the horse was not ridden by witches any more. (Preston, English)

Holy Days

My husband walked three miles before sunrise Easter Sunday to get dogwood to make crosses to put over the door. Some put crosses on the sill and some on the side of the door. (Cornwall, English)

From ninety years back were the witch years. In the night something would come and pull covers off three young girls in bed in a house on the back road and run cold, ice-cold, hands over them. They didn't know what it was. Even their father and mother didn't know. Their father took a butcher knife to be put under the pillow, and their mother put a Bible under her pillow, and after that they weren't bothered. Mother used to tell it about three young girls in that house. (Seabright, English, German and Scotch)

Put dogwood in two pieces and drive together with new pins like a cross and put it above every door and window in the house before daybreak on Easter morning. This will keep the witches out. (Eagle Head, German and English)

Religious Symbols

Christian doors made with panelling that forms a cross were made that way to keep the witches out. (Centreville, English)

Heat

My father was ploughing in Scotland when a witch came along and put a spell on the horses and he said they dropped down dead. He'd heard all you have to do is to get a piece out of a

74

witch's skirt and burn it under the nose of the horses. So he followed the witch and cut a piece out of her skirt and came back and burned it under the horses' noses, and the horses jumped up and went on ploughing. (Middle Musquodoboit, Scotch)

A Hex That Worked

An old man in Burin, Newfoundland, was born in a manger on Christmas Day like our Saviour. He had second sight and had the right to go on every ship for a mug-up. So many people went on board for mug-ups that a rule was made forbidding them, so Uncle Billy put a hex on one of the ships and it went out and was wrecked. They are afraid of him now and he gets his mug-up. (Ship Harbour, English)

Glooscap

Glooscap we meet in the very dawn of creation. He was the Master and at his dawn he lay on his back, prone, head to the rising sun and feet to the setting sun, left hand to the south and right hand to the north. This wonder-worker is not Nikskan, Father of Us All, nor Kesoolkw, Our Maker, nor Espae Sakumow, the Great Chief, but he was par excellence, the Micmac. He was co-existent with creation. After the seventy-times-seven nights and seventy-times-seven days appointed, there came to him a bent old woman born that very noonday sun. She was Nogami, the grandmother, and she owed her existence to the dew of the rock. Glooscap thanked the Great Spirit for fulfilling his promise.

On the morrow at the noonday sun a young man came unto Glooscap and Nogami. He owed his existence to the beautiful fall of the waters, and Glooscap called him Nataoansem, my sister's son.

When another morrow came and when the sun was highest, another person came unto the three who saluted and said (Indian name) took my children. This was the mother of all the Micmacs. She owed her existence to the beautiful plants of the earth. So there we have the Genesis of the race.

The Master himself retained the monopoly in stoneware, the toboggans, knowledge of good and evil, pyrotechnics and all other commodities until the time when the plenteous others had arrived. He shaved the stone into axes, spear points and other forms, but the braves preferred plucking the beard to scraping with one of his razors. He got fire by rubbing two sticks together for, well, perhaps two weeks. Knowledge of all sorts was his. He towered over the animals and the elements. On one occasion, when engaged in bringing all the wild, ferocious animals under the control of man, he changed the big monster into the squirrel for refusing subjugation. Another brute that depended on the thickness of his skin and the depth of his flesh to ward off men's weapons came to grief, as his pride deserved, and his bones to the end of time are to be a sign that pride will stand only for a moment. After a rest of seven moons Glooscap got busy clearing the rivers and lakes for navigation. It does not appear that he sublet the contract, and from all evidence obtained he had learned the truth of the saying, "If you want work well done, do it yourself."

In giving instructions for canoe-making before he left for the happy hunting ground, he cautioned his people not to venture out on the ocean. Father --------, who died in 1762, attests to the extreme precaution of the Indians when a canoe voyage of some consequence was to be made. This caution was no doubt traditional, and hence it was that only the rivers and lakes were rendered safe for navigation. Hunting and fishing were arts in which Glooscap excelled and he must have had a few good walkers to his credit. The traditional boy with the bent pin was like a tyro compared to this talent of Glooscap's that learned how to make a hook out of a bird's breastbone and a line out of the fibre of a ----- bush.

As early as 1629 the first shrine in America to St. Anne was erected. From henceforth St. Anne was to be called our grandmother by the Micmacs, and her first abiding place was near Nigonish, or Ingonish, in the county of Victoria, Cape Breton, and is still called St. Anne's. . .

76

* * * * * * * *

Well now, about this great Glooscap (the Indians' demi-god), what he had told to his people before he left this province after he had taught them of a good many different things; "My dear good childrens, now I'm going north and I'm going to fix your house because your house is distroubled here. Your home is distroubled. You'll now be living with white people which now will deal with gold and silver and (in) years to come, you will deal with the same thing." But the Indians didn't know the colour of gold nor silver, but they had known the name of the two different things.

"Well now then, I am going to leave after I've shown you everything that I want to show you. Now then, your home will be taken. Your province will be taken by those people which you are going to live with them. But I am going to build your home way up north where nobody else can come and live there but you. And your home what I am going to make up there, it will be so good, and it'll be mountains of gold that will be surrounded by your homes and it's nobody can get there but yourselves. But in years to come you will formally think, our province is all taken by those palefaces, but that will not be so. I will come and see the fair play, and I will come to see how that you will hold your homes and your province, 'cause the province is yours. It is nobody (else's) growth, prevail my words."

And all the things that he had reference to the growth of the people, it all came so exact, so truly, but this here coming back, it never has arrived yet, but we are expecting it. No doubt we certainly do believe that he will come and everything (be) dealt with according to the truth, and so therefore now the white people had reached from here to the Klondike, and they had gone on them mountains and canyons where they had discovered a lot of gold. (Library of Congress recording 2853, Chief William Paul, Shubenacadie)

Indian Legend

An Indian used to be here at North Gut and he had a point of land on the shore which was sacred land. It is believed that an ancient manitou came here at the end of every week to spend the weekend. One night he came too late and slipped, breaking the earth away. Now there is a cove the exact shape of a man's foot and it is supposed to be the footprint of this great spirit. (St. Ann's, Scotch)

Fairies

Stories of the little people are told very seldom these days, but the few instances we have prove that belief in their presence is not completely foreign to our soil. As a child I had often heard of fairy rings and sometimes in our play we would see a circle in the grass and someone would say, "Look, there's a fairy ring." We would view it curiously and then pass on because nothing ever happened, but it was supposed that this was where they danced at night. To us, fairies were happy and brought good gifts and it was a shock in later life to learn that in some countries they were considered evil . . .

There was one fellow one time was cutting a stick of wood and there were hills, you know, among the woods. You could see smoke under the hills long ago. They knocked down a big tree (and it) struck on top of these hills in the woods, built of clay. They heard (voices) underneath the ground (saying), "Oh dear, my hedge is hurt." They said again, "Oh dear, my hedge is hurt."

After a little while one feller says, "I wish I had a drink of buttermilk." There were two of them cutting, and after a little while out came a fairy with a wooden dish full of buttermilk. He says, "Do you want a drink? Here's the buttermilk you were talking about." But the feller who wished he had the buttermilk wouldn't drink, but the other feller drunk all he could of it. And the feller that didn't drink the buttermilk, he didn't have any luck afterwards, but the feller that drunk the buttermilk, he had luck long's he lived. He was happy in the world. (Sugar Loaf, Scotch)

Dreams

Dreams have come from the informants' interest rather than my own because in my investigations it seems that dreams have different interpretations for different people. For instance, many people think that a dream of horses foretells death, but if another person dreams of horses he will probably see one when he first looks out the window in the morning, or horses will come up in conversation during the day. A man in Mahone Bay had this latter kind of dream and got very excited when his wife read a letter from their son in Belgium after the Second World War who had written that they had plenty of everything except potatoes. His father thumped his fists upon the table and shouted, "My dream is out," for he who seldom dreamed had the previous night been in his sleep back on the farm where the harvest had yielded everything but potatoes. And incidentally, it is considered good luck when your dream "comes out."

My father wanted to learn to swim but his brothers thought he was too young and wouldn't teach him. One day he told them he could swim because he had dreamed how and he jumped off the wharf and swam like a frog. They were scared to death. (Allandale, English, Scotch and Irish)

Informative Dream

I dreamed that I saw a deer in the field and that it was standing facing me, I woke up and told my wife, "I'm going out to shoot a deer." My wife said, "You must be crazy." I told her I dreamt I saw a deer and I was going to get him. It was two o'clock in the morning so I went out and up the field and there I saw the deer exactly as he was in my dream and I shot him. (Gabarus, English)

Prophetic Dream

The evening before you came with that thing (tape recorder), I dreamed of beautiful songs coming to me one after another. It was so clear it made me full funny in the head. It must have been a forerunner of all the songs I was to sing into it for you. (Glen Haven, Welsh and German)

Other Dreams

Dream of the dead, hear of the living. (Dartmouth, English)

If you look out the window you forget your dream. (Broad Cove, German)

To dream of losing a tooth is to lose a friend. (Dartmouth, English)

Superstitions

People enjoy having what they call their pet superstitions, odd beliefs which for some unexplainable reason seem to act in their behalf. Indeed they give rather a pleasurable zest to life. Other people, however, distress themselves by looking constantly for signs and omens and will go to great lengths to forestall an ill-fortune they think may be approaching them. It is a true saying that superstition follows whom superstitions follow.

To say *pig* on a fishing vessel is a sure sign of a breeze; you must call him Mr. Dennis. (Lunenburg, German, where it is most widespread; West Pubnico, Acadian French; Glen Margaret, English; Clarks Harbour, New England)

If you say *pig* it makes the wind blow. Call it Little Fellah. They would never say pig when the men were out at sea. (Clarks Harbour, New England)

Sailors in the Canadian navy often have a pig tattooed on the knee. The rhyme is:

Pig on the knee
Safety at sea. (Devil's Island, English and Irish)

Ships and the Sea

Money was put under the masts of ships when being built to bring prosperity. (Allandale, English and Scotch)

I talked to Mr. Don Oland (H.C.)
We put money under both masts, a ten-cent piece (*Bluenose II* is a replica of the fishing vessel *Bluenose* — famous as undefeated champion in schooner races between Canada and the United States, and whose picture is on the back of the Canadian ten-cent piece), a silver dollar and a Spanish piece of eight which had been given by a friend. Various members of the family were there at the time, and the money was put in place by my father (Colonel Sidney C. Oland of Halifax). She was launched in 1963, stern first and she swung around so that her bow was facing the open sea. In Lunenburg (where she was built) this is considered a good omen. Also there was a thick fog that morning and it looked as though we might have a downpour at any moment, but about fifteen minutes prior to the launching the fog burned away and the sun came out. This was another good omen. Seamen don't like a black suitcase and when we ran into a heavy gale on our first voyage they searched the ship to see if anyone had brought one on board. If they'd found one they were going to throw it over the side.

Always turn a ship with the sun. It is bad luck to turn her against the sun, even if it takes a long time to do it the other way. (Tiverton, English, Irish and Scotch)

Never turn a ship to the left, always to starboard, back out and turn starboard. (Lunenburg, German and English)

Don't whistle on a ship; it is bad luck. (Yarmouth, English; Victoria Beach, English, Irish and Scotch)

A woman in a boat is bad luck; however one night we had a woman with us and we caught fifty-two pounds of halibut. We sold it, she bought some, and we ate it, so there was no bad luck about that. (Port LaTour, New England)

Fishermen won't have bluebirds on the wallpaper of their houses, and they don't like greeting cards with bluebirds on them. (Clarks Harbour, New England)

All seagulls are old sailors. (Dartmouth, England)

Knit hair in the toe of a man's stocking: that will bring him back. (Shag Harbour, New England)

Don't launch a boat on a Friday or start a trip on that day. (Gabarus, English; Bear Point, New England)

Friday was a day to be frightened of. Once the twenty-ninth of February came on a Friday, and that was a day to be very much frightened of. (Brooklyn, Irish and Scotch)

Mining

A miner would never tell the day he was going to stop work for fear that day would bring an accident. (North Port Mouton, Irish)

In gold mining they would never allow a woman to go down a mine. (Kentville, English)

On the thirteenth miners don't like to go down. I've heard of Tommy Knockers (familiar among Cornish miners) having been heard before an accident. Men have often seen lights before an accident and they would quit and come up. Before Christmas if one was killed there seemed to be three. That was a bad time for accidents; they always seem to happen at that time. In Stellarton if miners heard a certain tapping in the mine they would come up and close it down and stop work for that day. (Springhill, English)

Seasons

Don't hang a calendar up before the New Year. It is bad luck. (Dartmouth, Windsor, English; Lunenburg and New Glasgow, German)

82

Lunenburg people won't let a woman in first on New Year's morning. The best luck comes with a dark-haired man carrying a piece of wood. (Conquerall Banks, German)

A (servant) maid from the eastern shore said that in her home Epiphany is still known (1929) as Old Christmas and all Christmas decorations must be taken down if bad luck is to be avoided, and Roman Catholics must go to church. (Dartmouth, English)

Bake bread on Good Friday and take a bun and put it away. It will never mould or never spoil, but it will dry up and get hard. It is supposed the ship you sailed in or the house you lived in would never be lost or burned. The one bun will last a lifetime. (Spry Bay, French and Portugese)

On Hallowe'en Night go down the cellar steps backwards and look in a mirror and you will see the face of your future husband. (Lunenburg, German)

Christmas

Between Christmas and Epiphany, accept Christmas cake in any house you enter; each house where it is eaten will give a month of happiness in the coming year. (Dartmouth, English)

Oxen kneel at Christmas. One time some men were coming home from town and down went the horse with his knees on the road. It was ten or eleven o'clock. Cattle and horses kneel. (East Petpeswick, English)

Animals, Insects and Birds

When a cat washes its face company is coming. (Sherbrooke, English)

To keep a kitten from wandering, rub its forepaws with butter. (Dartmouth, English)

If a bumble-bee enters the house, a stranger will call. (Terence Bay, French and English)

If a spider crawls on you you will get something new (to wear). (Ostrea Lake, English)

A cricket in the house is good luck. (Annapolis Royal, English, Irish and Scotch)

It is bad luck to kill a ladybug: pick it up and put it out the window. (Dartmouth, English)

Birth

When a baby smiles in its sleep, angels are passing overhead. (Dartmouth, English)

If you were born with a caul, your house will never burn down, don't destroy it. (Clam Harbour, English)

Something always happens to help a person born with a caul; they will never want, so should never worry. (Annapolis Royal, English)

People born with a caul can see things (second sight); as long as the veil is in the house, the house won't burn down, and a ship will never be lost if a veil is aboard. Seamen sometimes ask people who have them to sail with them. One man was asked to sail once for that reason but he had a feeling the ship would be lost on that voyage and he didn't go. The ship sailed and was lost. (Victoria Beach, English and Irish)

Death

In some parts of the north end of Halifax when people visit a house of death they always put a hand on the body. This goes back to the time of Julius Ceasar when, if a murderer touched a corpse, the wound would bleed. The custom may show that the person never bore the dead person any ill will in life. The psychology is that if you had hurt him in life, you would never go near him in death. (Auburn, English)

Good and Bad Luck

Never put new shoes on a table; it is bad luck. (Annapolis Royal, Dartmouth, English)

If money rolls away from you it is good luck, and if you find money, you mustn't give it away; it is lucky money. (French Village, French)

Always leave some money in your purse so it will never be empty. (Dartmouth, English)

Don't give anybody anything that is sharp or pointed without receiving a penny in exchange; otherwise it will cut friendship. (Dartmouth, English)

Never open an umbrella in the house. (Dartmouth, English; general)

Water Divining

To find a spring (of water) use an alder branch. This is often done but the branch will only move for certain people. (Blanche, New England)

Kenny Thorne demonstrated how to find water with an alder branch. He held the branch at arm's length from his body in a firm grip with the thumbs down straight and other fingers tightly holding the forked limbs. He walked over marshy wet land and nothing happened, but, when he went over the only dry part in sight, the rod bent forward until presently it was pointing straight down. As he moved away again, still holding it, the branch came up once more in his hands and we could see where the bark had come off the limb from being twisted in his hands. It was an exciting experience in the half-dark of the evening. Emma Laurence and I tried it but it wouldn't move for either of us, nor for Mr. Casey. The branch bends only above running water and so strong a grip is held on the Y-shaped alder branch that it may take the flesh off the hands when it turns completely over.

To find the depth of ground to be dug before water appears, the man now walks slowly backwards, still holding the branch with the single end pointing down. It will now start to come up and he will keep walking until the forked end points down again. This Mr. Thorne did, counting off the distance, which was three feet. By this he knew that after digging three feet water would appear.

$$\lambda \qquad Y \qquad \lambda$$

Position 1   Position 2   Position 3

(Victoria Beach, Irish and Scotch)

Home Remedies (Tuberculosis)

Dr. Rabain was an old French doctor who came around here when mother had been given up with TB (tuberculosis). He was said to have been stolen by the Indians when a small boy and he had learned their cures. Father asked him to come and he said he could make a cure. He always asked twenty dollars down and twenty dollars when the patient was well again.

"Now," he said, "we'll go into the woods and gather the herbs." So they made six gallons by steeping them in water, and one gallon of liquor with sugar and raisins. This was supposed to last a year. He told her she would think herself cured in six months, but she must keep the treatment up for the full year.

He made her two jackets of tarred oakum sewed together and they had to be changed every day and washed in salt water with the tide going out. He said the moon controlled the tide and the moon controlled the body. He told her she must have warm fresh air, and that she mustn't go out after two o'clock as there was a certain dampness in the air she wouldn't feel, but it was there. He stayed for three weeks. She had to eat certain foods like spiced bush tea. He used to put old Jamaica rum with the herbs to preserve them. Mother lived to be eighty-four. The doctor always ordered more liquor for preserving the herbs than was necessary, and drank it up while here. He taught her the cure and she has used it effectively since. One old man called him in and wouldn't pay the fee so he said, "You can die and be damned," and he did. (Allendale, Scotch and Irish)

Planting Crops

Cucumbers are planted the day before the full of the moon. Everybody who plants them that day has better luck. On the decrease of the moon, plant things that grow underground, crops like peas and beans in the full of the moon. (East Quinan, Acadian French)

Plant anything that grows underground in the dark of the moon; anything that bears on top of the ground on the increase of the moon. (Milford, Annapolis County, French and Dutch)

One man here would only plant his potatoes in the forenoon, never in the afternoon. (Mahone Bay, German)

Always sow cabbage seeds on Good Friday. (French Village, French)

The fourth of July, wet or dry, plant turnips. (Cheverie, Scotch)

Excerpts from
A Life in
Folklore

Helen Creighton's autobiography, *A Life in Folklore*, was published in 1975. It offers 244 pages of detailed incidents and pictures, beginning with her birth on September 5, 1899 and covering seven and a half decades of her life, offering a wealth of chronologically-arranged memories and teeming with characters.

Helen demonstrates her storyteller's art on the first page when she speaks of being born with a caul. A caul? She describes it and the almost magical properties ascribed to it in succeeding pages. Indeed there are occasional references to it in this and her books of folklore as she learns from others of the high regard felt for a caul in superstition and folklore.

Helen is able to trace family origins back to their beginnings in this country, bringing bygone days to life in the process, as she focuses on her ancestors. With the respect she has acquired for roots she takes pride in being of the sixth generation on both sides of her family.

Secure and sheltered as the youngest child, Helen's perception of life was dramatically widened on that catastrophic day in December, 1917 when Halifax and surrounding area was shattered by a devastating explosion. Her vivid recollections of that dire event seem to be 'a must' for inclusion here. Towards the end of her account of her own experience at that time, she mentions being approached by a man at the Ferry Wharf who offered her a copy of a newly-written poem of first-hand impressions of the Explosion.

Glancing at it she found it extremely gruesome and shudderingly waved it away. In later years she bitterly regretted that impulsive reaction as she would have given much to find a contemporary song about the Halifax Explosion. She mentioned this in *A Life In Folklore*, which gives rise to an interesting sequel.

While I was researching material in The Helen Creighton Collection at the Provincial Archives of Nova Scotia for this book, I came across a stained and torn printed sheet with the heading, "Halifax In Ruins." It bore twenty-five four-line verses full of explicit, harrowing descriptions of the city in the aftermath of the Explosion. No author or date was given, only the information that it was sold by R.M. Martin, Boatman, Ferry Wharf, Halifax, N.S. I eagerly checked this with Dr. Creighton, who told me that after the publication of *A Life In Folklore*, nearly sixty years after the Explosion, a woman who had read it sent her a copy of the poem. Whether this first-hand, on-the-spot account had ever been set to music or sung I was unable to discover. Probably not, but what a unique addition such a ballad would be to the folklore of the region.

A Life In Folklore is a continuous narrative which makes it somewhat difficult to excerpt, since one episode flows naturally into the next. The way Helen was guided and led along her path of destiny makes fascinating reading, as does her single-minded dedication to her self-determined career, a career in which there were no trail-blazers and few guidelines. *She* was the trail-blazer. Fortunately, she frequently encountered helpful people who made large or small individual contributions to her lonely endeavours; scholars, singers, musicians and boatmen, electricians and telephone linesmen, cameramen and film and radio technicians, professors, porters and politicians, fishermen and their families, coal miners and lumberjacks, cottage wives alert to prompt their singing husbands and who unfailingly produced refreshments at the end of a long evening of recording. These all come alive in *A Life in Folklore*, for Helen Creighton has a superb and accurate memory and a generous appreciation for all those who helped her along the way.

Personal Experience of the Halifax Explosion

On December 6, 1917 at approximately nine o'clock in the morning I was awakened by what seemed to be a heavy blast. Doris Davis, whom I had met on my West Indies trip, was staying with me. We sat up and saw towards the northwest a great ball of fire in the sky. Then came a terrific explosion. Was it the sixth sense inherited with my caul, my guardian angel, or what that caused me to shout, "Duck, Doris, duck," so that we quickly slipped under the bedclothes? Glass from four windows and plaster from the ceiling descended upon us and part of the window casing with the nails down was imbedded where my head had rested upon my pillow. Like everybody else we thought a bomb had fallen and fled to the cellar. Every step was over broken glass but miraculously our bare feet didn't get a scratch. Mother had a slight abrasion over one eye, otherwise we were untouched. She was anxious about my father who had gone to Halifax, for by now we knew there had been a great explosion. Doris and I volunteered to find him. We dressed hastily, shaking tiny fragments of glass from our shoes for it had penetrated everywhere. Then we ran to the ferry. Dartmouth ferries have a remarkable record and not even this calamity stopped them although blood and broken glass was everywhere.

My father loved a spectacle and like other commuters that morning had been watching the great columns of smoke billowing from the burning *Mont Blanc*. Her cargo of munitions had ignited after a collision with the Belgian Relief Ship *Imo*. Father declared afterwards he was the only one on the ferry dock left standing, but it is unlikely he had any idea what he did. From the habit of a lifetime he made his way to his office on Bedford Row, and when we found him a teen-aged boy was helping him clear away the rubble of plaster and broken glass.

Then word came to run south, that another explosion would follow ten times worse than the first. Father wouldn't budge, but promised to leave shortly and insisted that Doris and I go on. We knew mother would worry, but daren't return by ferry and instead followed the crowd to the Gorsebrook Golf Links at the edge of town. Here sick people were lying out of doors wrapped in blankets against the cold and everybody was in a state of bewilderment. Before long we heard that the crisis had passed: ammunition at the Halifax Dockyard was under control. Back at father's office we learned that he had gone to Citadel Hill, the worst possible place if another explosion had happened, and had met there a Presbyterian minister clutching his one remaining child by the hand. His wife and other children were dead. I can picture them, both dazed, and trying to help one another. On the return trip we talked to two men from the *Niobe*, our one naval ship stationed in Halifax and docked close to the scene of the explosion. One had been blown from the ship to the jetty, but fortunately was unhurt.

By the time we arrived home, I realized that though I had been caught up in the general excitement, it was now time to consider others. Consequently I got the car out and started downtown to offer help wherever needed, but there was so much glass on the street that in no time I had a flat tire. Three men helped, and by the time it was changed a distraught Mr. McAulay asked if I would take his family to his contractor's shelter in Halifax. They had been at Tuft's Cove where the destruction was as devastating as in the north end of Halifax, and he had only been able to get them this far. One daughter had pneumonia so we stopped at Dr. Dickson's office but he had heard that one of his north end patients was dying and had left in a hurry. A nurse was dressing a woman's face. She was fortunate because many people with cuts could get no attention and for the rest of their lives carried streaks where falling soot had mingled with blood in their wounds. I delivered Mrs. McAulay and the children while he searched for bedding and on the way back I had the good luck to see my brother Sydney who had brought a company of engineers in from McNab's Island where he was stationed. They were putting tents up on the Commons, and I was able to tell him we were safe.

On the return ferry I took on another assignment. A mother and child were being taken by horse-drawn cart to the Nova Scotia Hospital on the Dartmouth side, probably because Halifax hospitals were filled to overflowing. There was no room for the sailor accompanying her and the child on the cart where the woman was lying flat. I was asked if I could drive them and first take the mother to see a doctor. Dr. Dickson assured us the mother would live so I drove slowly to the hospital with the team following. There were a number of discharged patients standing in the hospital doorway so I was given a young man whose face and head were bandaged from the nose up, a mother and infant and a girl about fourteen badly cut, and a man in agony because in addition to his own wounds, his wife and child were missing, and he was now in the care of two soldiers. After delivering the man with the bandaged head at Thistle Street, I had to go to North Dartmouth. All along Windmill Road buildings were burning, and all the north end of Halifax, seen clearly across the harbour, was either in flames or smouldering. As we neared Tuft's Cove I saw that spruce trees had fallen across the road and wondered if I would be able to take the mother and child all the way. Mercifully there were no more flat tires and it was a great relief when we came to a little green one-storey house and they were home safely. By now darkness had fallen and the only illumination came from infrequent car lights and burning buildings. On the way back I was glad to take soldiers in who had been doing rescue work all day, they filled the car and stood on the running boards outside and hung on. The young girl was still with me because the Fairbanks Street house where she had been staying had been abandoned, and I said we would put her up for the night.

Tired out, I was thankful to return home. Father and mother had been hanging grey camp blankets at the windows all day against the cold and otherwise making the house habitable. But the girl didn't want our hospitality and begged to be taken to her home in Eastern Passage, and father, who loved to drive, thought he would like the six-mile trip. Doris went with him. Time went by and they failed to return. We were filled with anxiety aggravated by the fact that we had no telephone communication. Eventually they arrived by taxi. There had been another flat tire and father had been unable to cope with it. We were touched by the appearance of Mr. Ellsworth Smith, our carpenter, who dropped in to make sure we were all right for the night. We had lost one hundred and six panes of glass. This would include the small panes in which windows were often divided, the winter's double windows, and perhaps some of the panes from the greenhouse. Much of the plaster had fallen and chimneys were damaged. Picture frames were studded with tiny fragments of glass, and to this day we are finding pieces of glass that ooze up from the soil. Some fifteen hundred people were killed and six thousand wounded by the explosion. The world was shocked because heretofore it was our men who went to battle who were killed. Now for the first time women and children, the aged and infirm, were victims in their own homes.

Fortunately for me, though not for other people, it snowed the next day and I could rest with a clear conscience. Then we heard that volunteers were needed in Halifax and the next day Doris and I offered our services to City Hall. We were soon off on a house-to-house canvass, and at noon theatre players at the Academy of Music gave us a welcome meal. That afternoon as we were coming off duty we got a ride on a horse-drawn wagon where we met a young woman who had lost everything. Wearing little under her coat and with nothing on her feet but rubbers, she was in search of clothing for her children. We took her to the Green Lantern Building where we got outfits for her as well as the children, and then to Cogswell's store to get thawed out. I can still see her patient selfless face — we thought her a noble character.

One regret stays with me. As I was sitting in the car one day waiting for the ferry, a man approached with a sheet of paper in his hand with a song on it about the explosion. He wanted to sell it to us. I took one look and saw a line which read, "There lies a little baby's hand and there an old man's head." I gave it back in a hurry and we laughed at anything so gruesome. Little did I know the time would come when I would scour the land for someone with a song of the explosion. I found one in 1933 and another twenty years later, but I have never come across that ballad sheet, or indeed any other. Words (and music) which may be the very ones I rejected in 1917 are in my *Maritime Folk Songs*, taken down from two singers so many years later.

First Radio "Aunt"

In those happy days I should have been looking for a husband, but life was too exciting to settle down . . . I began to write seriously, favouring poetry, . . . I also wrote for children and had written a book-length story called *The Tale of the Golliwogs.* Fortuitously, when this was finished. Radio Station C.H.N.S. was set up in Halifax and two of the men read bedtime stories to children. Sensing an opening and having my own story on hand, I applied for that job and got it.

In 1926 I was "Aunt Helen," the first station "aunt" in Halifax and probably in Canada. I read from my book, made wooden golliwogs for those who wrote in, wrote all the dialogue for the half-hour show, found the music, and was paid, by the *Herald and Mail*, two dollars a broadcast.

Introduction to Folk Music

Why I selected Dr. Henry Munro, Superintendent of Education, I can't remember, but on a late spring day in 1928 I called on him. We talked of many things and then he showed me a book just off the press, *Sea Songs and Ballads from Nova Scotia* compiled by Dr. W. Roy MacKenzie from Nova Scotia's north shore. It contained one hundred and sixty-two songs with copious scholarly notes and forty-two melodies. Dr. Munro held it proudly in his hands and suggested I might do for the rest of the province what Dr. MacKenzie had done for the River John and Tatamagouche areas. "If you could find only one ballad," he said, "your fortune would be made." It was eventually, but not with money. At that time I didn't know what a folk song was. At school we sang the "Mapul Leaf our Emblum dear," and other patriotic songs which, incidentally, we loved. He suggested I take the volume home and study it, and what happened next seems more than fortuitious.

. . . I was invited to a picnic at Eastern Passage at the entrance of Halifax Harbour . . . we found a villager, Mike Matthews, . . . and in that easy way one does in the country, we began to talk . . . I said, "Has treasure ever been found along this shore?"

"Yes," he said, "a boy came to a farmer one day with a penny in his hand and when the farmer rubbed it he saw it was a double loon . . . He asked the boy where he got it, then sent him on an errand. As soon as he was out of sight the farmer dug, and that family has lived comfortably ever since . . . the old people will tell you about that . . . They'll tell you stories and sing you songs as well."

"What kind of songs?"

"Pirate songs," he said. Well, if the stories were too incredible, I could write about men who still sang pirate songs, so I asked Mike where to go. "To the end of the land (now Hartlan's Point)," he said. I asked him to advise the Hartlans of my coming, little realizing that a great new door had opened and that the Eastern Passage road had become my path of destiny . . .

Path of Destiny

Should I go on now with children's stories and magazine articles, try my hand at fiction, or make this my vocation? Then I remembered the Dominion Graphologist's reading of my handwriting in Ottawa and the observation, "You are the investigative researcher type." Was this right? Even with my inexperience in folk music, I knew these were good songs and sensed they should be written down.

Tales Incidental to Songs

Richard Hartlan loved to spin tales. He would say, "If it's a lie I'll tell you, and if it's the truth." When he talked of ghosts and witches, pirates and wrecks, he would look solemn and his eyes would grow round with the marvel of it all. A tall tale or song of exaggeration he would dub a foolishness song, and his face would light up as he looked for our response. Fortunately, I wrote everything down, mainly I think because it seemed to please them, but also because I hoped that some day I would see a way to use it, which of course I did.

One of the most lovely songs in my whole collection, "When I Was in My Prime," a variant of the English "Seeds of Love," came from Enos, and I never hear it now without thinking of him. Richard's greatest pride was in "The *Flying Cloud*." He remembered seventeen double verses.

Scholars Excited

By the end of a year I had a sizable collection, and Mr. Murray Gibbon, Chief Publicity Agent for the Canadian Pacific Railways who was then putting on folk festivals in western Canada, paid me sixty dollars for ten pirate songs. I took the rest to Dr. Archibald MacMechan, head of the English Department at Dalhousie University . . . As he read, he grew excited and sent for Dr. McOdrum, a young professor who had just taken his Ph.D. in ballads in Scotland. Both assured me I had some rare treasures, but what should my next step be?

Discovering Child Ballads

From 1882 to 1898 the late Professor Francis James Child published in five great volumes all the variants he could find of what he called the English and Scottish Popular Ballads. Highly dramatic, the songs give little description of the characters who are easily pictured from their actions. These rare and ancient songs became known to scholars as Child ballads and with a little experience are easily recognized. Many have gone out of oral tradition, so I considered it a great feather in my cap to be able to find any here. In time, of the 305 so designated, the Maritime Provinces have given me variants of 43.

Nicknames

. . . I added to my supply of nicknames, each with a story to explain why the person was connected with the distinguishing noun . . . We have Hughie the Hide (he tried to steal one and was caught). Fourteen (he changed a cheque from $1.40 to $14), the Skunks (they painted their boat black with a white stripe which gave someone the idea), Angus the Bird (he flitted about from place to place), Signboard Alice, Angus Shoot the Cat, Rory the Lover, Billy Sunday (not the great evangelist, but one who bootlegged on Sunday), Kitty the Basket (nothing so innocent as eggs and butter in *her* basket, no, she carried a bottle), Sarah the Goat (her father was Dan the Goat), Rory Cold Day, Murdoch the Mortgage, Boxcart Sadie, Galloping Sue, Kitty the Pullet, Hughie the Rooster, Duncan the Flea and the Seven Daughters. Two MacDonald sisters worked in the Antigonish library and were known as The Professors. You would never say, "Are you going to the MacDonalds' this afternoon?" but, "Are you going to the Professors'?"

My Songs Broadcast from England

In 1938 the usual way to hear folk song programs was by short wave radio from England since we had few, if any, here. These were listed in our papers, and when I read that Canadian songs would be on I thought, "I wish they knew ours." My radio was upstairs where I heard it announced that there would be songs in English, French, "and finally from Nova Scotia where Helen Creighton has discovered — " I didn't wait for the rest but ran downstairs to tell the exciting news, for this had never happened before. We crowded round the radio. The voice would fade and static interfered but we heard enough to realize this was a lovely voice and the choice of songs was to my liking. The singer was Eve Maxwell-Lyte and the next day I wrote her the first fan letter she ever received.

Four Thousand Sons?

There were miners at Inverness, and I felt they too would have songs. When we saw one walking home with his lunch box we offered him a ride. I said, "Have you miners' songs down here?" and was delighted when he said, "Yes, we have a lot of them." I said, "What are they like?" He looked so surprised that I said, "How do they go?" To this he answered, "Mine are here." That seemed a strange remark so I said, "Who sings them?" Then he began to laugh, "Did you say songs? I thought you said sons." In Montreal many years later my songs and sons got mixed up again when a newspaper stated that I had four thousand sons!

Gaelic Saves the Day

The story is told of a Gaelic-speaking woman who married a French husband who knew no Gaelic. A man named McCrimmon used to visit her when her husband was away, and one night the husband was heard coming home unexpectedly. Houses had huge fireplaces then, so she told him to climb inside, which he did, but he left his feet dangling. As her husband came in the door she picked the baby out of its cradle and walked up and down singing in Gaelic:

> Pick up your feet McCrimmon, McCrimmon,
> Pick up your feet McCrimmon my boy.

A New Era

A new era began in 1949. No more great Presto machine to carry, no more converter and batteries, no great box of blank discs and no more sapphire needles to break, for tape recording had come in, and the Museum had its own machines. I must have looked pleased with life on the first day I used mine, for I

99

got two proposals of marriage from singing farmers I had never met before.

. . . Maida Parlow French joined me for a visit to the island home of another author, Evelyn Richardson, author of *We Keep a Light* . . .

When the boat was anchored we clambered aboard a small skiff. Mr. Richardson had made a skidway where boats were drawn up by motor power, an ingenious rig, as fishermen would say. Then we walked half a mile over a wide road with spruce trees on either side, surf on the sea side and blue flags in bloom on both sides. Everywhere were signs of loving care. Mrs. Richardson was painting the interior of the house, and the morning passed in animated conversation. We picnicked in the lee of the lighthouse with a gentle summer mist caressing our brows. She gave us macaroni and cheese, lobster salad, wonderful homemade bread, the best peas I've ever tasted from the garden, and for dessert bake apple, a small fruit that grows in a few places along the coast . . .

Big Moments

Two big moments in 1950 were the arrival of proofs of my second book of music, *Traditional Songs from Nova Scotia*, and *Folklore of Lunenburg County* in its final book form. I went shortly afterwards to a tea at my brother Syd's house and a guest got hold of a copy and refused to take his nose out of it all afternoon, taking the food offered him automatically and scarcely lifting his eyes from the book, a grand sight for an author. Included in this book are a number of stories of witchcraft which I got in a surprising manner. I knew it had been practised in that county and said one day I could believe in ghosts but not in witches. This proved a challenge and they explained that there are witches in the Bible and that it is written "Thou shalt not suffer a witch to live." Then stories came easily.

Ballad Dramatized

It was in the year 1950 that I saw my work used in an original and dramatic way. At Hubbards the Adult Education Department put on a concert in which they included the ballad of "The Farmer's Curst Wife." On one side of the stage a group sang the story. On stage acting the words were the farmer, the devil, the shrewish wife and, in a corner, four other devils. When the wife "up with her foot and kicked out their brains," down the four went, and when "three little devils peeped over the wall," up came three more heads. You will recall that the story is about a woman who was taken to hell where she proved such a nuisance she was taken home again. With a good tune and a whistling chorus, there was scope for all kinds of original treatment. Another time the same group dramatized the folk song "Gallows." They had a gallows on stage and the hangman dressed in black stood beside a waiting noose. The clergyman, also in black, was there. The young man approached his doom and hesitated as singers offstage sang,

> As he went up the first steps of the gallows
> His own dear father he chanced to see.

At the next step it was his mother and so on. As he went higher the tension grew and I was glad I knew that on the final step his sweetheart would appear with his pardon. One child who didn't know the ending screamed. Since ballads are action stories they lend themselves to this type of treatment and all that is needed is the skill to portray them visually.

Broken Ring Becomes Folk Opera

I had never envisioned a folk opera based upon our songs, but in 1953 this happened when *The Broken Ring* was presented in Halifax by the Nova Scotia Opera Association with music by Trevor Jones and libretto by Donald Wetmore. Words and music were woven into the story practically unchanged. There are over twelve hundred songs extant on the theme of a ring broken between lovers when parting. The man returns, usually after seven years, and in disguise tries to woo the girl. When he finds her faithful he reveals his identity through his half of the ring and she swoons in his loving "arrums." The Halifax Symphony played the Overture in its 1954-55 series and CBC radio produced the full opera in 1956 beginning with Mrs. Gallagher's clear unaccompanied voice singing the first verse. It then lay dormant until Dartmouth High School students took it for their centennial project and were invited to perform it at Expo '67 in Montreal.

Healing Hands

Folklore came in for a practical testing then, for I developed neuralgia in my left cheek. In Stewiacke I often dropped in to the home of Reverend Kennedy Wainwright. When the pain was severe, Mrs. Wainwright said, "Would you like Kennedy to put his hands on your face? He often does it for us; we think he has healing hands." He did this and, I suppose, said a short prayer. The pain didn't stop immediately but began shortly afterwards to decrease, and in a week or two it was gone. A few years later it returned so I asked him to do it again. This time he took it more seriously. The family gathered around and we all said our little prayer. The pain failed to develop further and I've never had it since.

Ghostly Encounters Common

When people nowadays say they couldn't sleep after reading *Bluenose Ghosts* I say, "That's fine; I couldn't sleep after writing it." All that summer I tried to write for one hour at least, but I would get so absorbed it often ran to more. The chapter on devils I found particularly disturbing and was careful not to make it bedtime writing, but a good deal was written at night and it was probably the exhilaration of getting on with the job more than fright that kept me awake. There was new material everywhere, and many of the stories were collected while writing the book. Although Nova Scotia is particularly fertile ground, it seems that no matter where we are in the world, if five people are together and the supernatural is mentioned, at least one will have had an experience for which there is no explanation. People keep these things to themselves for fear of being laughed at. Sometimes they have seen a loved one after death and they have been comforted and don't want anybody telling them it is just their imagination activated by grief.

A Gracious Hostess

It must have been nearly an hour before Mr. Gillis and the children joined us, and the room was soon spellbound as one song followed another. All the while, Mrs. Gillis, a gracious hostess, sat on the piano stool in apparent enjoyment. But even though he was an excellent singer and I wanted to make the most of the opportunity, by ten o'clock I felt I could work no longer. They wanted to make us tea then, but the Morrisons refused as our hosts had so many children to put to bed. I was surprised they were dissuaded so easily because it is almost a point of honour for a Cape Bretoner to serve tea to guests. Then because the day's work was well done, the evening fine and warm, the company congenial and the road unfamiliar, I relaxed my usual speed and dawdled home. Two days later Mr. Gillis appeared at the Morrisons' door.

"You nearly had a picnic on your hands the other night," he announced. "Just before you came my wife said she was ready for the hospital. When you left we followed you to Marion Bridge but didn't like to pass in case you'd think you'd kept us from something. Then we raced to Sydney and an hour later the baby was born." This was hospitality carried to the nth degree and that's the nearest I ever came to being a midwife.

Astral Travel?

For some years I had worried about my papers which had accumulated through the years and needed weeding out, and I pitied my executors if anything happened to me before I could do it. One night I felt myself going up like an astronaut, only at a much slower speed. I was startled and thought, "I'm dead. I've just died." At that point all the cares and worries, some of which I didn't even know I had, seemed to drop away, and I had the most wonderful feeling which must be like the Biblical peace which passeth all understanding. Then I thought, "The poor people who will have to look after my papers," and back I came. It was probably a dream, but I will never really know. However, if that is what dying is like then we can take heart.

A Best Seller

When I finished writing *Bluenose Ghosts* I began to have misgivings. How would the public receive such a book? I can't remember ever hearing a ghost story told at home, but I do remember my mother on several occasions saying that she had once been told she would make a good medium. Although she seemed impressed by this information, it never went further than that, and I have no idea where this opinion of her originated. I had read little on the subject, partly because ghost stories frightened me, partly because I wanted to present the Nova Scotia viewpoint with an unbiased mind. Before submitting it for publication, I asked my good friends Phyllis Blakeley, archivist, Marion Moore, historian and newspaper correspondent, and Doane Hatfield, teacher of high school English, . . . to read the manuscript. They all voiced approval and suggested minor changes, each reflecting their own activity. With these revisions I sent it off, never dreaming I had written a best-seller. It has had ten printings.

It is strange that stories of the supernatural, something I looked upon as something purely incidental to my main work, should perhaps be my best effort. It is difficult to compare the two fields since songs and stories are so different, but my book has certainly reached many people, and it has helped them to discuss their own unexplainable experiences. To this day I receive telephone calls or letters sharing some strange event. From the book have come radio and television interviews, radio dramas based on its stories, two long profile-type television shows in colour, and so many invitations to speak that I have to turn most of them down, for they take too much time from writing. Children tell me their teachers read from the book in school. At social gatherings or even when out shopping, people I scarcely know come up and discuss the subject. Having had a number of strange things happen in my own life, I suppose I am in tune with the subject. A few who had kept things to themselves for as long as thirty years now feel free to talk, and at times I have been able to help them. I never dreamed I would be a consultant on the supernatural.

Bluenose Ghosts on Radio

My ghosts were put to a new use in October of '61. Animated drawings were made by the CBC's gifted staff artist, Harry Orenstein. The story was called *The Box* and dealt with a duel. To anyone not accustomed to ghost stories it must have been spine-chilling. They had written a script which I read as the story unfolded. I find the use of my material exciting and inspiring, especially when it takes such a variety of forms. But CBC Halifax did us a great disservice where our songs were concerned. When the sort I was collecting were at the height of popularity, they ran many programs of folk songs "from here there and everywhere," but never from here except for "The Cherry Tree Carol" and "Farewell to Nova Scotia." I never felt there was anything personal in this, but why were they so short-sighted as to ignore their own heritage, especially when many of our songs are of equal merit to, if not better than, most? It was hard to work at times under such discouragement.

Supernatural Warning

On my way to the Miramichi Folk Song Festival in 1963, I had stopped off for a night's rest at Marshlands Inn, the nicest place of its kind in the Maritime Provinces, . . . I decided to sleep in the early evening and go downstairs later for cocoa which is always served at bedtime, and where there are always interesting people to be met. I had wakened and was getting out of bed when I saw a vision of myself coming towards me, but as a child of ten with a very sweet and welcoming expression on my face. I recognized this immediately as the worst omen I could have and put my hands out as though pushing it away. It faded but returned almost immediately but not quite so vividly. Again I made the gesture of pushing it away. It came a third time, but by then was quite faint. I got up and went downstairs as planned, determined to forget it as I always react when something supernatural occurs. I met the other guests as though nothing had happened and afterwards had a good night's rest.

In the morning it began to bother me and I felt I must drive with extra caution. I had kept especially alert when going through a wooded section and had come to a clearing when suddenly, directly in front of my car, I saw a deer. It seemed to have come from nowhere. Isn't it extraordinary how much the mind can think of in a split second of time? I said to myself, "There's a deer, I can't miss it." Then I prayed fervently, "Oh God, *please* help me," and because I believed this possible, I took my hands off the steering wheel. There was a crash — that was inevitable — but I was not propelled forward as I would expect after colliding with a heavy object at fifty miles an hour, not did the car swerve off the road, but came to a gentle stop. With shaking knees I got out to survey the damage for I had heard the sound of glass being shattered. The right headlight and lens were broken in many pieces and the metal below the light was pierced. I looked for the deer but it had disappeared, and even though I backed up there was no sign of it. Were it not for the evidence, I would have thought the whole thing an illusion. I concluded that the vision coming as a child and not an adult, had not been a death omen but a warning. The conclusion was strengthened the following spring when on the train between Toronto and Winnipeg I heard the porter singing and talked to him about Negro songs. We then got around to folklore, and among other things he mentioned that his mother had said a person born with a caul would always have a warning before danger. He of course had no idea I was born with a caul, so it is odd that he mentioned it.

The Gift of Grace

When my sister Lilian died in 1968, I had the most amazing experience, and one that still gives me comfort and joy. Usually when I was worried about her I could feel my parents around, but when I held my lonely vigil in the Tatamagouche hospital, I had no feeling of their presence and missed them. I had gone to church myself to say special prayers for her, but as the moment of death approached, I realized no clergyman had been asked to visit her in hospital. I must have looked stricken as I rushed to the nurse on duty.

Reverend James Fraser came quickly, and as he stood on one side of the bed and I on the other, the two attendant nurses left. He read a passage from Scripture, said a prayer for the dying and one for me. I didn't realize until later that she had probably stopped breathing during his prayer for me. She was certainly alive when he started. When he was through we sat for a moment in conversation until I realized that the shoulder that had been pulsating with her rapid breathing had ceased its motion.

What happened during the prayer for me was an inflow of strength so vigorous that I knew it would sustain me through the days ahead. In fact it sustained me for most of the following year. I learned later that this is known as the gift of grace. The theological meaning is "strengthening influence" or "divine regenerating." It uplifted me in a way I had never known, like a benediction, and I was in a state almost of ecstasy. Since then I have never thought of her with relief as at the dropping of a heavy burden, but always with love and affection, and usually I find myself smiling. At first I used to feel her close as though things were reversed now and she was looking after me, and one time in that period between waking and sleeping, I saw her. It was just her head. She looked happy and seemed to be flying slowly through the air at the centre of a little group I can only think of as a heavenly host.

"A Goodly Heritage"

Now in 1975 I see our songs used in textbooks in Canada and abroad. Many have been arranged for solo and choral singing and appear in sheet music; others are combined with melodies from Newfoundland for orchestral playing. I am especially pleased that locally we have a band number composed by Kenneth Elloway, choral arrangements by Mona Maund, Eunice Sircom and others, and harp arrangements by Phyllis Ensher. We have two symphonies by Klaro Mizirit, conductor of the Atlantic Symphony Orchestra, and one by Alex Tilley as well as a mini-opera by Steven Freygood. Dave Woods and Dennis Farrell have made compositions from our melodies for Gary Karr which he plays on his extensive travels, and when the Men of the Deeps perform in China this year, our songs will be in their repertoire. From *Bluenose Ghosts*, the Nova Scotia Photographic Department has just released a twenty minute film using the title of the book and having stories performed by Neptune Theatre actors and actresses. It will be distributed by the Nova Scotia Tourist Bureau. At the St. Francis Xavier spring convocation I was given the honorary degree of Doctor of Letters, and at Dartmouth Natal Day celebrations there was a presentation of a gold medal. Now mindful of a rich, full life I can say in the words of the Psalmist, "The lines are fallen unto me in pleasant places; yea, I have a goodly heritage."

Some of the Songs and Their Singers

Helen Creighton began her search for folksongs in 1928 and since then has collected thousands. No anthology could offer more than a fragment of this massive body of work. The fragment here consists of eight songs selected mainly to illustrate the diversity and range of her endeavours. They were chosen in consultation with Clary Croft, well-known singer of folk songs and folklore specialist, who is also the Contract Archivist of the Creighton Collection at the Public Archives of Nova Scotia. It was no easy task to narrow this selection to so few. They are:

> Cherry Tree Carol, A & B
> Broken Ring Song
> Drimindown (Three versions)
> The Red Mantle
> Nova Scotia Song
> The Sauerkraut Song
> Cecilia (English and French versions)
> The Blackbird

Dr. Creighton had a great respect and a high regard for her singers, a talented band of individuals who enabled her to preserve a disappearing facet of life in the region. As many of the songs are associated in her mind with one particular singer, their voices from years ago still sing in her head. She has recorded not only the songs, but some of the distinctive qualities of the singers.

The "Cherry Tree Carol" is one of the best-known folk songs; it has the distinction of being a Child ballad. This version comes from the black community and was sung for Dr. Creighton by Mr. William Riley of Cherry Brook. At the time he was eighty-six years old, blind and deaf. He was a very religious man and sang with great feeling, especially songs which envisioned the bliss of the heavenly home. His grandfather had been a slave and Mr. Riley would weep when he sang songs of slavery, one of which was "The Auction Block," an outstanding addition to Helen Creighton's folk songs. A musical production entitled "The Collector," based on Helen Creighton's work, was presented at Mount St. Vincent University in 1982. It featured the "Cherry Tree Carol." One of the singers was Mr. Riley's great-granddaughter who sang this beautiful song with equal feeling.

There are many versions of the "Broken Ring Song," which is based on a popular theme in folk music, lovers separated, each having half of a broken ring. When the man returns after a seven-year absence his beloved does not recognize him, but demonstrates her constancy. This song was the basis for a folk opera written by Trevor Jones and Donald Wetmore which was performed at Expo '67 among other places. The version given here was sung by Mrs. Edward Gallagher of Chebucto Head, a singer, who, with her family, was the source of many songs for Helen Creighton.

"Drimindown" is variously a milking song, a lullaby and a lament, depending upon the singer's predilection. Apparently it was known far and wide as is evidenced by the different versions given here which were received from three different singers, Mrs. Jas. Creelman of Dartmouth, Capt. Charles Cates, a former Mayor of Vancouver when on a visit to Halifax, and Mr. Ernest Sellick of Charlottetown, Prince Edward Island. Mr. Sellick recalled that his father would sing this song as a lullaby as he rocked his children on his knee. The chorus in Irish Gaelic gives this an added interest.

In contrast with the three previous songs, "The Red Mantle" came from just one singer, Mr. Angelo Dornan. Hearing that Dr. Creighton was collecting songs in New

Brunswick, Mr. Dornan wrote to her, saying he remembered a few old songs his father had sung. Because of pressure of other things, it was a year before the collector got back to him. Of Irish descent, Angelo Dornan was a farmer at Elgin, New Brunswick. He had returned to his native province after spending many years in western Canada where he never heard an Atlantic folk song. His father had been a lumberman and had picked up many songs during his years in the woods. He frequently sang them at home and his son's wonderful memory retained them for over forty years when he was far from home. When he began singing them for Dr. Creighton the 'few songs' flooded back in their entirety and expanded to become one hundred and thirty-five, some of them never obtained from any other singer. They comprise a large portion of *Folksongs From Southern New Brunswick.*

The "Nova Scotia Song," also known as "Farewell To Nova Scotia," might well be the one ballad Helen was told at the beginning, that, if she could but find it, would make her fortune! Perhaps, if not a fortune, it could alone ensure that her work would endure, for it has become so popular it seems to have acquired a status of the unofficial anthem of Nova Scotia. A great many singers knew this one, each with an individual rendition. It was particularly well-known along the eastern shore where it was sung in the schools. Helen Creighton first heard this song over fifty years ago and combined a number of variants to produce the version given here. When the Queen visited Nova Scotia she heard this song and enquired if it was a Scottish air. Later research revealed that this song did indeed have its origins in old Scotland where it seems to have been a soldier's farewell, rather than a sailor's. "The Soldier's Adieu," by Robert Tannahill (1774-1810) was originally published in 1808. Dr. Creighton sent this information to the Queen and received a letter of appreciation from Buckingham Palace. The "Nova Scotia Song" has engendered interest, not only in folklorists, but in musicians, film-makers, writers, historians and the whole cultural community. It became a film in October, 1986, made by Glenn Walton for The Atlantic Film Maker's Co-operative. It features a group singing this most popular of folk songs on Devil's Island. Writer Marjorie Whitelaw researched the background of the song and wrote an informative article about it for *The Nova Scotian.* Pipers play it at government functions and it is enthusiastically greeted at the annual Tattoo and was sung in the Great Hall of the People in China.

"The Sauerkraut Song," whose words are given in the excerpts from *Folklore of Lunenburg County* has the distinction of being indigenous to the south shore of Nova Scotia, it does not appear to have roots in any other land, as most of the songs do. Helen Creighton took down the words from singer Japhet Dauphinee while her friend, Doreen Senior, transcribed the music.

We are indebted to another ethnic group for "Cecilia," which is an Acadian milling song. The English words given here are hitherto unpublished. A variant of the French version was published by two Capuchin monks in *Chansons d'Acadie.* The students of Petit Etang school sang this for Helen Creighton in 1944. We are indebted to the Creighton Collection of the P.A.N.S. for permission to include it here.

"The Blackbird" is also published here for the first time, according to Clary Croft, who is very fond of this delightful song and has included it in some of his own public performances. I was privileged to hear the original recording and found it very moving. The almost identical voices of the elderly Armstrong twins, singing in unison, almost a quarter century ago, have a most appealing quality. This recording is a gem, one of many preserved for posterity by the dedicated efforts of Helen Creighton.

The Cherry Tree Carol (A)

Then Jo ~ seph took Ma ~ ry up
on his right knee Say-ing Ma ~ ry won't you
tell me when the birth day shall be, — Say-ing
Ma ~ ry won't you tell me , when the birth day shall
be.

Reprinted by permission of McGraw-Hill Ryerson from <u>Traditional Songs From</u>
<u>Nova Scotia</u>

Sung by William Riley   Transcribed by Roy Bauchman

114

Cherry Tree Carol (A)

1. Then Joseph took Mary up on his right knee
   Saying Mary won't you tell me when the birthday shall
   be, —
   Saying Mary won't you tell me when the birthday shall be.

2. "The birthday shall be on that old Christmas night
   When the angels in the glory rejoice at the sight
   When the angels in the glory rejoice at the sight."

3. Oh Mary walked in the garden just like a little child,
   Saying, "Give me some cherries for I am beguiled,"
   Saying, "Give me some cherries for I am beguiled."

4. Joseph said to Mary, "I give thee no cherries,
   Let the man give you cherries who did you beguile,
   Let the man give you cherries who did you beguile."

5. Then the tree spoke unto her and it began to bow,[1]
   Saying, "Mary gather cherries from the uttermost limb,"
   Saying, "Mary gather cherries from the uttermost limb."

Sung by Mr. William Riley, Cherry Brook (Negro)

1. In one singing he said, "The tree hearkened to him and it began to bow."

Child says that this carol is highly popular and is derived from the Gospel of Pseudo-Matthew, Chapter 20. Williams says it also occurs in the Coventry Miracle Plays. Sharp tells us that the references to the birthday do not appear in the English texts, but in two of his variants from the Appalachian Mountains it is given as the fifth day of January. Mr. Riley gives it as Old Christmas Night. Sharp explains that in 1751, when a change in the calendar had become expedient, eleven days were dropped out between September 2 and 14, 1752, thus making January 5 the date of Old Christmas Day. In 1800 another day was taken from the calendar, and in 1900 still another, so that Old Christmas Day now falls on January 7. Library of Congress recordings: William Riley and Nina Bartley Finn.

The Cherry Tree Carol (B)

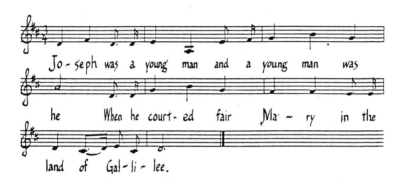

Jo-seph was a young man and a young man was
he When he court-ed fair Ma ~ ry in the
land of Gal ~ li ~ lee.

Reprinted by permission of McGraw-Hill Ryerson from Traditional Songs From Nova Scotia

Sung by Annie C. Wallace
Transcribed by Roy Bauchman.

Cherry Tree Carol (B)

Joseph was a young man and a young man was he
When he courted fair Mary in the land of Galilee
When he courted fair Mary in the land of Galilee.

Sung by Mrs. Annie C. Wallace, Halifax

The Broken Ring Song

As a sai-lor walk - ed all in a gar-den A pret - ty fair maid he chanced to spy. It was for to view her he stepped up to her and said "Fair maid can you fan-cy I" ?

Reprinted by permission of McGraw-Hill Ryerson from *Traditional Songs from Nova Scotia*

Sung by Mrs. Edward Gallagher
Transcribed by Roy Bauchman

Sung by Mrs. Edward Gallagher, Chebucto Head.

The ancient theme of the returned lover and the part played by a ring is one of the oldest as well as most widespread motifs in folk ballad and folk epic. Variations of the theme are well nigh innumerable. In English ballads the theme occurs in "Hind Horn," "The Kitchie Boy," "Katherine Jaffray," etc. Classic examples are the myths of Odysseus, Agamemnon and Diomedes. In most of these songs the lover returns in disguise and tests the fidelity of his sweetheart, producing at last the half of the ring she has given him. It is sometimes known as "Seven Years," seven years being the usual time of parting, not only in the English but in European and Scandinavian ballads as well. Among other broken ring songs in this volume are "The Dark-Eyed Sailor" and "Lovely Nancy."

Broken Ring Song (A)

As a sailor walked all in a garden
A pretty fair maid he chanced to spy,
It was for to view her he stepped up to her
And said "Fair maid can you fancy I?"

2. She said "Seven years since my life has left me
And seven years since I did him see,
And seven more I will wait upon him,
Perhaps he'll come back and marry me."

3. "Perhaps your lover he is married
And is enjoying wedded bliss,
Or perhaps your love he is dead and buried,
The heavy ocean rolls o'er his breast."

4. "If he be married I hope he's happy,
If he be dead I wish him rest,
But for his sake I will never marry,
The reason why is I love him best."

5. "Oh, what if I be your single sailor,
The one you don't expect me to be,
Oh, what if I be your single lover
Who has come back to marry thee?"

6. "If you be my single sailor,
The one I don't expect you to be,
Show me the ring that was broke between us
And when I see it I will believe."

7. He put his hand all in his bosom,
His fingers being both brown and small,
He pulled out the token between them broken
And when she saw it down she did fall.

8. He picked her up all in his arrums
And said, "Fair lady I'm none the worse,
For I have plenty of gold and silver,
The cruel ocean I'll no more cross."

Drimindown

There was an old man and he had but one cow, And
how that he lost her he could-n't tell how, For white was her fore-head and
slick was her tail And I thought my poor Dri-min-down ne-ver would fail.

Chorus:
E - go so ro Dri - min-down ho ro ha,
So ro Dri mindown nea~ly you gra, So ro Dri-min down
or~ha ma dow Me poor Drimindown nea le sko che-a go sla-ni-gash
So ro Dri-min down ho ro ha.

Reprinted by permission of McGraw-Hill Ryerson Limited from Maritime Folksongs.

Sung by Ernest Sellick   Transcribed by Roy Bauchman

Drimindown
1. There was an old man and he had but one cow,
   And how that he lost her he couldn't tell how,
   For white was her forehead and slick was her tail
   And I thought my poor Drimindown never would fail.

Chorus
   E-go so ro Drimindown ho ro ha, So ro Drimindown
   nealy you gra,
   So ro Drimindown or — ha ma dow Me poor
   Drimindown nea le sko
   che — a go sla — ni — gash So ro Drimindown ho ro ha.

2. Bad luck to you Drimon and why did you die?
   Why did you leave me, for what and for why?
   For I'd sooner lose Pat and my own Bucken Bon
   Than you my poor Drimindown, now you are gone.

3. As I went to Mass one fine morning in May
   I saw my poor Drimindown sunk by the way,
   I rolled and I bawled and my neighbours I called
   To see my poor Drimindown, she being my all.

4. My poor Drimon's sunk and I saw her no more,
   She's sunk on an island close down by the shore,
   And after she sunk down she rose up again
   Like a bunch of wild blackberries grown in the glen.

(Bucken Bon was the name of his wife; Pat was his son)
Sung by Mr. Ernest Sellick, Charlottetown, P.E.I.
September, 1956.
The chorus is Irish Gaelic and has been written down as it
sounds.

Drimindown

Here it is a Milking Song, and sung as a lullaby by Mrs. Jas. Creelman, Dartmouth, in the early 1930s:

1. As I was walking one morning in May
   I met my old Rooniedown down by the Bay,
   So white was her face, so slick was her tail
   I thought my old Rooniedown never would fail.

Chorus:
   A gush and I drew me down r awa',
   A gush and I drew me down mumbly ga,
   A gush and I drew me down r I couldn't,
   I say goodbye to this land.

And here are the words used by Capt. Charles Cates when Mayor of North Vancouver, on a trip to Halifax, August, 1956.

Tape 166A

O Drimindown lived before she was dead,
She gave me fresh butter to spread on my bread,
Likewise good milk for to stiffen my crown,
And now it's black water since Drimindown's gone.

Chorus:
   Ah ha Drimindoon ar a draw,
   Ah ha Drimindoon addle you draw,
   Ah ha Drimindoon hook a sook O
   My Drimondoon deary oh where have you gone?

2. Drimindoon, Drimindoon, for which and for why?
   Drimindoon, Drimindoon, what made you die?
   So white was your milk and so slim was your tail
   I thought my poor Drimindoon never would fail. *Chorus*

Mr. Sellick and Captain Cates sing it as a lament.

The Sauerkraut Song*

Permission of Public Archives of Nova Scotia - Helen Creighton Collection

Sung by Japhet Dauphinée.
Transcribed by Roy Bauchman

* words on page 30

The Red Mantle

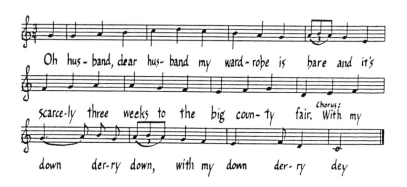

Oh hus-band, dear hus-band my ward-robe is bare and it's

scarce-ly three weeks to the big coun-ty fair. With my

down der-ry down, with my down der-ry dey

Creighton, Helen. _Folksongs from Southern New Brunswick_. National Museum of Man Publications in Folklore, No. 1. Ottawa: National Museums of Canada, 1971 p. 213.

Sung by Angelo Dornan
Transcribed by Roy Bauchman

The Red Mantle

1. "Oh husband, dear husband my wardrobe is bare
   And it's scarcely three weeks to the big county fair."

Chorus:
   With my derry derry down,
   With my down derry dey.

2. "Oh times they are hard and wages is low,
   Provisions are scarce as you very well know." *Chorus*

3. "Oh husband, dear husband grant me my desire,
   Get me a red mantle to wear to the fair." *Chorus*

4. "Between now and harvest I will do my best
   To get you a red mantle as well as the rest." *Chorus*

5. He got me the mantle so costly and rare
   And I gayly set out for the big county fair. *Chorus*

6. I thought that the likes of me wouldn't be seen there
   that day
   But green mantles were worn and carried the sway.
                                              Chorus

7. The costly red mantle in shreds I did tear
   And I went home in tears from the big county fair. *Chorus*

Sung by Angelo Dornan, Elgin, New Brunswick.

NOTES
This song has only come from Mr. Dornan, and I have not seen
it in any collection. He has recorded it for Folkways record
FM 4006, "Folk Music From Nova Scotia."

(From *Folksongs From Southern New Brunswick*)

Nova Scotia Song

collected by Dr. Helen Creighton

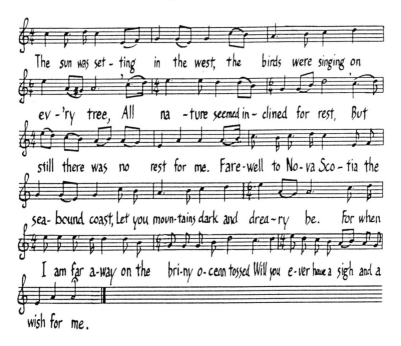

The sun was set-ting in the west, the birds were singing on ev-'ry tree, All na-ture seemed in-clined for rest, But still there was no rest for me. Fare-well to No-va Sco-tia the sea-bound coast, Let you moun-tains dark and drea-ry be. For when I am far a-way on the bri-ny o-cean tossed Will you e-ver have a sigh and a wish for me.

Nova Scotia Song

This seems to be particularly well known in the Petpeswick and Chezzetcook districts, where they tell me it used to be sung in the schools. This effect of the sea upon the lives of people in remote fishing villages can be deeply felt. I have combined the variants to make one song, taking them from the following contributors: Mr. and Mrs. Thomas Young; Mr. Garvie Young; Mrs. Dennis Greenough, Petpeswick; Mrs. James Owens, Chezzetcook; Mrs. Annie C. Wallace, Halifax; and Mr. Ben Tupper, Scott's Bay. The melody is from the singing of Mrs. Dennis Greenough.

Library of Congress recording: Walter Roast.

1. The sun was setting in the west,
    The birds were singing on ev'ry tree,
    All nature seemed inclined for rest
    But still there was no rest for me.

Chorus:
    Farewell to Nova Scotia the sea-bound coast,
    Let your mountains dark and dreary be
    For when I am far away on the briny ocean tossed
    Will you ever heave a sigh and a wish for me.

2. I grieve to leave my native land,
    I grieve to leave my comrades all,
    And my aged parents whom I always held so dear,
    And the bonny, bonny lassie that I do adore. *Chorus*

3. The drums they do beat and the wars do alarm,
    The captain calls, we must obey,
    So farewell, farewell to Nova Scotia's charms,
    For it's early in the morning, I am far, far away. *Chorus*

4. I have three brothers and they are at rest,
    Their arms are folded on their breast,
    But a poor simple sailor, just like me
    Must be tossed and driven on the dark blue sea. *Chorus*

Cecilia

Mon père n'a-vait fil- le que moi, Mon pèr' n'a-vait fil-le que moi, Des-sus la mer il m'en vo ya Sau-tez, mig-non-ne, Cé-ci- li- a. Ah! Ah! ah! ah Cé-ci- li-a! Ah Cé-ci- li- a ah! ah!

Permission of Public Archives of Nova Scotia ~ Helen Creighton Collection

Sung by children of the Petit Etang School
Transcribed by Roy Bauchman.

128

Cecilia

1. My father had only one daughter, (bis)
   Across the sea he sent me.
   Jump, my sweet, Cecilia.
   Ah ah ah ah Cecilia Ah Cecilia, ah ah

2. Across the sea he sent me, (bis)
   The sailor who took me there,
   Jump, my sweet, Cecilia.
   Ah ah ah ah Cecilia, Ah Cecilia ah ah

3. The sailor who took me there, (bis)
   Fell very much in love with me,
   Jump, my sweet, Cecilia.
   Ah ah ah ah Cecilia, Ah Cecilia ah ah

4. Fell very much in love with me, (bis)
   Often he approached me,
   Jump, my sweet, Cecilia.
   Ah ah ah ah Cecilia, Ah Cecilia ah ah.

5. Often he approached me, (bis)
   And said to me in a silly way,
   Jump, my sweet, Cecilia.
   Ah ah ah ah Cecilia Ah Cecilia ah ah

6. And said to me in a silly way, (bis)
   "My dear one, kiss me,"
   Jump, my sweet, Cecilia.
   Ah ah ah ah Cecilia Ah Cecilia ah ah

7. "My dear one, kiss me," (bis)
   "No, no sir, I would not dare,"
   Jump, my sweet, Cecilia,
   Ah ah ah ah Cecilia Ah Cecilia ah ah

8. "No, no sir, I would not dare, (bis)
   Because if my father knew of this,"
   Jump, my sweet, Cecilia.
   Ah ah ah ah Cecilia Ah Cecilia ah ah

9. Because if my father knew of this," (bis)
    Jump, my sweet, Cecilia.
    Ah ah ah ah Cecilia Ah Cecilia ah ah.

       Sung by nine girls and three boys at the Petit Etang
school; this song is traditional here and the Acadian version
has been published by two Capucin monks in Chansons d'
Acadie but with slight differences. Recorded for the library of
Congress in 1944. The song is also on Reel 181B with Peter
Chiasson, Grand Etang, taking the solo parts, and on National
Film Board documentary "Songs of Nova Scotia," 1958.

© Helen Creighton and the Creighton Collection of P.A.N.S.

L.C. 205B
Mt. A recording No. 16

Cecilia

Mon per' n'avait fille que moi,
Mon per' n'avait fille que moi;
Dessus la mer il m'envoya,
Sautez mignonne, Cecilia.
Ah! ah! ah! ah! Cecilia! Ah Cecilia, ah! ah!

2. Dessus la mer il m'envoya: (bis)
   Le marinier qui m'y menait . . . Sautez, etc.

3. Le marinier qui m'y menait; (bis)
   Devint fort amoureux de moi; . . . Sautez, etc.

4. Devint fort amoureux de moi; (bis)
   Souvent de moi il s'approchait . . . Sautez, etc.

5. Souvent de moi s'approchait; (bis)
   Et me disait d'un air niais . . . Sautez, etc.

6. Et me disait d'un air naiais; (bis)
   — Ma mignonnette, embrasse-moi . . . Sautez, etc.

7. Ma mignonnette, embrasse-moi; (bis)
   — "Non, non, monsieur, je n'oserais . . . Sautez, etc.

8. Non, non monsieur, je n'oserais, (bis)
   Car si mon papa le savait . . . Sautez, etc.

9. Car si mon papa savait . . . Sautez, etc.

© Helen Creighton

131

The Blackbird

I once knew a maid - en whose for - tune was
Chorus: Then if I was a black - bird I'd whist - le and

so, She court - ed a sail - or, a young sail - or
sing I would fol - low The ship that my true love sailed

boy, she court - ed him dear - ly by night and by
in, and on the top rig- ging I'd there build my

day Un - til this young sail or he sailed miles a -
nest like an eag - le I'd fly on his lil - y white

way.
breast.

Permission of Public Archives of Nova Scotia ~ Helen Creighton Collection

Sung by Allister and Judson Armstrong
Transcribed by Roy Bauchman

The Blackbird

1. I once knew a maiden whose fortune was so,
   She courted a sailor, a young sailor boy,
   She courted him dearly by night and by day
   Until this young sailor he sailed miles away.

Chorus:
   Then if I were a blackbird I'd whistle and sing,
   I would follow the ship that my true love sailed in,
   And on the top rigging I'd there build my nest
   Like an eagle I'd fly on his lily white breast.

2. My true love is handsome in every degree,
   My parents despise him because he loves me,
   But let them despise him or say what they will,
   While there's life in my bosom I'll love the lad still. *Chorus*

3. If I was a scholar, could handle a pen,
   There is a trying letter to my love I would send,
   I would tell him my sorrows, my griefs and my woes,
   If I could but find him I would crown him with gold.
   Chorus

Sung by Allister and Judson Armstrong, Sherwood, Lunenburg Co. Recorded by Helen Creighton, June 23, 1949.
   The Armstrong brothers are twins, about 65 years of age. When Judson's throat gets tired from singing he asks for salt which he eats to clear it. This seems to have the desired effect.

Two New Tales

Anyone interested in folklore or folk music would find much fascinating material in the Dr. Helen Creighton Collection in the Public Archives of Nova Scotia. Throughout her life, Helen Creighton has been a preserver of the written word, hence the Collection contains such items as her school scribblers, early poems, notes of appreciation written by the girls she taught in Mexico when she was little more than a teenager herself.

There are clippings, letters, different copies of the same folk song, musical notations made in the field, story ideas and memos of incidents related to her by phone callers; published and unpublished material.

In the unpublished category is an entire book manuscript on the folklore of Grand Manan, islands Helen visited during a summer collecting in southern New Brunswick. With her permission, and that of the P.A.N.S., "The Destitute Family and Mr. Locke," taken from that manuscript, is published here for the first time.

Although Dr. Creighton did not do extensive collecting in Prince Edward Island, she did acquire a number of folk songs and a few stories from that province, one of which is related here. It seems to have a lot in common with tales found in *Bluenose Magic*. "Witch Story" is another tale from the Dr. Helen Creighton Collection never before published. I am grateful to Dr. Creighton and the Public Archives of Nova Scotia for this privilege.

The Destitute Family and Mr. Locke

. . . This story was started after the first German war. Hard times struck Grand Manan about two years after the war was over, and it was in the month, I think, of October that things was pretty tough on Grand Manan. You couldn't get anything to eat; you couldn't get anything from the stores without you were strictly honest so this is the way I'll start the story.

It was in the month, I think, of October when I had my garden stuff all in the cellar and snugged up for winter, and I had two bags of potatoes that I didn't sell. Didn't know but I might sell them through the winter. But anyway, this night my wife was settin' up, going to cook a pan of bread, and I said to her, "I guess I'll go to bed," and the children was all playin' round, so I went upstairs and started for bed, and I had taken one leg out of my trousers when I heard children crying, and I hollered down to my wife and asked her what was the trouble downstairs — what were the children crying about. Well she says, "There's no children crying. You must be out of your mind. Are you hearing something?"

Well I said, "I heard something alright 'cause I heard children crying." Well I might have set there a half a minute more or a minute more when I heard the mother say, "Children I'm getting you something to eat. Don't cry. I'm getting you something to eat as fast as I can." Well then I knew that it wasn't my children so I put my pants on, come downstairs, and my wife had the bread in the oven. This must have been somewheres about nine o'clock at night as near as I can remember. Anyway I went down cellar and I took some of each and every thing that I had in the cellar. I took two bags of potatoes and I took carrots, beets, and all kinds of vegetables that I had, some of each, and I lugged them up and put them down by the cellar door and closed the door. I went to the barn and I harnessed my horse, a horse by the name of Rowdy with a white strip on his forehead.

I come down to the house and I loaded my cart up and my wife says, "Ashton you must be insane. For gracious sake if you take this food or these vegetables to anyone's house will you ask them — tell them — ask them if they are destitute. And

136

if they're not destitute beg their pardon and come home." So I says, "I will do that."

Well at the time when I had the cart loaded, and I got in the cart and started my horse up, I didn't know where to go. I had no idea where to go, but I knew I should go because I heard these children crying, and I was sure I did. So I started down the road. From my place when you get to the corner down here a short distance about fifty yards or seventy-five yards, there's a road running to Grand Harbour down by the cemetery, the back road and the other road goes right straight down by Mr. Small's service station. Before I got to this corner I heard a voice say, "Let the horse have his rein." Well that was good enough for me. I made up my mind that horse had to lead me where the home was destitute for something to eat and where I heard the children crying, so at every cross road I let the horse have his rein, and between these crossroads I started the horse on a little trot. When he got down to the service station he didn't go down the road toward Grand Harbour, but he went towards North Head and on my way to North Head the horse kept right on going over the road instead of going to Whale Cove or some of those other roads. He kept right on the main road going towards the steamboat landing.

Well he went over as far as the steamboat landing and took a road up by Mr. Lahey's store. Mr. Lahey's dead now. There was two Lahey's that had a store, one on each side of the road. My horse took the road that led to the left up this road. Well there was some lights burning along in people's houses, but it was getting late. It must have been somewheres around eleven o'clock when I got to North Head. Well when my horse got abreast of a certain house — I'm not saying what house it was or who it was — but when my horse got abreast of this house he put both feet right out straight forward, his fore feet right out straight and put them down hard and I says, "Get up Rowdy," and he wouldn't move, so I said, "This must be the place," so I got off my cart. I went to the door and I knocked. This house I never was in in my life, and these people I didn't know or wasn't acquainted with. Well I knocked at the door and a man came to the door and I said, "Mister, I've had a vision tonight and I've heard children crying (here the narrator's voice breaks at the poignant memory) for something

137

to eat, and I heard the mother say just as distinctly as could be, "I'm getting you something to eat as fast as I can." That's the words the mother said and that was good enough for me, so I'm up here tonight and I'd like to know if you are destitute, and if you are, you are welcome to what I've brought here, and if you're not, I will take it back home."

The man said, "What's your name?" I said, "My name is Ashton Locke." Well he said, "Mr. Locke come in."

Well I went in the house, and there upon the floor lay four little children. If I'm not mistaken there was two boys and two girls but I wouldn't say for sure. But anyway the children was laying on the floor to sleep. The mother was sitting there in a chair. They had on a hot fire and a boiler of water on the stove all boiling and a pot on the stove, and the man says to me, "Mr. Locke I've been all over North Head today and they wouldn't let me have a twenty-five pound bag of flour on time."

Well I said, "Mister, I'm sorry that anyone would be mean enough that they wouldn't let you have a bag of flour, but" I says, "you're welcome to what I got here in the cart," and I says, "come out and help me lug it in." So he did come out and he helped me clean the cart out, and I said to him, "This is the last time you'll ever come to want; you'll always have food from this time forth," and I guess as near as I can tell, they never wanted for anything after that. I sat there a few minutes and they talked and they went to work while we was talking peelin' potatoes and cleanin' carrots and putting them in the pot to cook and he thanked me for my kindness, so I told him I thought it was about time I was trying to get back home. It would be late when I got back home.

Well when I got back home it must have been two or three o'clock in the morning because I didn't trot my horse very much; it was quite a heavy horse. But when I got back home my wife was settin' up waitin' for me, and when I got my horse put up and come down to the house she asked me if I had found the place where anyone wanted food, and I says yes I did, I found the place. Well I've never mentioned this here place where it was; never told the family that was destitute but much as — oh I guess it must have been a year or two after that (here the narrator got a little mixed; it was probably a good twenty years) there was a woman came from Montreal to start the new

138

hospital at North Head. When she went away it happened as though that my daughter Katrina and myself was aboard the boat the same day that she went away. We was in a little place there in the boat, and I didn't think anyone else was in there except a young fellow was tellin' a story about savin' a boy off of the wharf there at North Head, but this woman told a story, seemed a true story, so I thought to myself now I'll tell a little story that happened to me. So I says — I started in to repeat the story before my daughter and this here nurse that was here to start the hospital at North Head. I started to tell the story, and in time I got it finished I didn't think there was anyone in the apartment besides my daughter and this here lady and this boy, fellow, young man, and then when I got my story finished I heard this cryin' and sobbin'. I turned around and there was a young woman sitting behind me that I didn't know was there, but she was there, and I said, "What's the trouble with you?" and she said, "My mother has told me the story so many times I can't help but cry." (The narrator's voice breaks again at this recollection). She says, "I can't help but cry, but mister don't feel bad because it's a true story. Every word is true what you're telling because my mother repeated it to me a good many times."

Well this lady that was the nurse from — that came from Montreal — she says, "That proves that what this man has told us is exactly true because there's the proof right behind, both her crying and telling us the same story, it's true, see?" I guess that's about all I can tell you, but I've never been in the house since and these children grew up and I don't know 'em when I see them. No. That's about all there is to it.

Mr. Locke, when you told it first didn't you say that the table was all set with the dishes?

Oh yes, the table was all set with clean dishes settin' on the table. The dishes was there, but nothin' in the dishes. I left that out. They didn't have nothin' to put in the dishes, only what I brought them. He couldn't get a bag of flour in North Head, so that's the truth as near as I can speak it.

Mr. Locke, when the woman said she was going to get them something as soon as she could, how did you realize from those words that she had nothing to get? Was it the way she said it?
The way she said it that I realize that she didn't have anything because the children wouldn't have been crying on the floor if she'd had anything to eat. She said, "I'm gettin' you something to eat as fast as I can," and she was settin' the table to make them believe that she was getting them something to eat, but the children was layin' down on the floor and cried themselves to sleep. I think she thought that someone would come and bring them something to eat. You know a mother can see ahead sometimes, and feels things too, you know. No I kinda think she had some kind of a little vision that there would be someone come.

And you say you took a load of bread when it was fresh out of the oven?
I took a loaf. I made my wife give me one loaf. She had three loaves in one — she had three loaves in the pan, so I got her to take off one loaf of bread and I put it in a paper bag and took that.

You have a farm. I suppose you have a pretty well stocked cellar, but you had a big family yourself.
I had a big family myself, but I had plenty for winter as far as vegetables and things.
I never see the children afterwards till I see this girl behind me that night. It must have been somewhere between eighteen or twenty years because it was a young woman that was behind me.

You told the young man in this story that he would never be in want again. Did you tell him that just to make him feel better, or why?
I told him that because I felt as though he'd never need food again. You know, he'd always be able to get plenty to eat after that, for him and his family. I could tell pretty well because I had that feelin'.

Have you had other feelings of that kind?
I've had all kinds of feelings. Yes, and that ain't the first trip I ever made over this island, different places, yessum.

So then your wife wasn't too surprised when you went off on a jaunt?
No, but on that racket that night she thought I was crazy. She found out afterwards that I wasn't as crazy as she thought I was.

(For another story in which a man goes on an errand in obedience to a strange request see *Bluenose Ghosts*, pp. 135-137).

Other Psychic Experiences of Mr. Ashton Locke:
My son's wife's mother, they gave her up and said she couldn't live. Three doctors gave her up, said she wouldn't live an hour, and I told my son's wife, "Your mother is going to get well and she'll be as well as she ever was in her life, and she has, and she's been teaching school now for three or four years, and that's not all; I've told different people things.

A man was cleaning up a lot and expected a woman to be brought home that night to be buried there and I told him — he was cleaning this lot up on Sunday and I told him, "You don't want to work on that lot because the woman is going to get well and she'll be here a good many times to this island. She lived away off the island but she always came here because this was her home and she was born here. And I said she'd come home and she did get well after the doctor gave her up, and she came back here to the island, oh I suppose half a dozen times, her and her sisters. They came to Grand Manan to visit the island here, and they had no hopes for her at all, so this man got miffed at me because I told him the woman was going to get better. He thought I didn't know what he was talking about. I did; I think I did.

(*Bluenose Ghosts* has a chapter devoted to people with the gifts of Foresight and Hindsight, pp. 69-90).

© Helen Creighton and the Creighton Collection, P.A.N.S.

Witch Story

This story was told by the people in Rose Valley where I was born. This incident I am about to relate now took place in a neighbour's house, . . . My story is going to be disjointed because I am going to try to recall it as I tell it to you.

It concerns a neighbour family of ours in the days of my grandfather who was having difficulty getting butter off the cream. They used to churn in those days with the old dasher churn. I've seen them in my boyhood days. The story as it was told to me was that they couldn't get the butter off the cream. I remember when I used to wheel this old dasher in the churn myself, the butter would be very hard to get. It was probably caused by the cream at the wrong temperature and that sort of thing. But this story insists that there were some occult powers used by some evil person with evil intent. Anyway, my neighbours couldn't get any butter off the cream or any butter in the churn. Somebody told them there was a man lived up the country some ten miles or so, which was a long ways to go in those days — transportation was slow — who could take this curse off the churn. They were told some evil person had put a curse, a bad wish, on the churn, and I remember this old neighbour lady of mine telling me in her kitchen, and she said, "This charm was actually on the floor in this kitchen where you're sitting now." This man came and he put it between his knees and he scalded it and he put certain kinds of rinses in it and he did some mumble jumble with his hands holding it between his knees; magic words or words that the average person couldn't understand. Finally he said, "Now lady, you'll get butter off that; you'll get butter off your churn." The story is that he removed the curse on the churn, and those people actually told me for a fact that after that, the thing worked all right and they got their butter. What he did probably goes back to old Scotch superstition, I don't know.

I lived in an area where they were all Scotch Presbyterians. My grandparents on both sides had come from Scotland at about the time when most people had come out from the old country. I lived a mile from the county line — the line between Queen and Prince county and on our side of the line I think they were all Scotch Presbyterians and immediately

142

on the other side of the line they were all Irish Roman Catholics. The old Scotch and Irish people were very clannish, but they visited back and forth and they worked together, but they were very very superstitious, and they had some beautiful old stories. Now these people actually believed that.

Told by Mr. Neil Matheson, Charlottetown, P.E.I. and recorded by Helen Creighton, Sept. 1956.